Bill Clinton

Michael Tomasky

Bill
Clinton

THE AMERICAN PRESIDENTS

ARTHUR M. SCHLESINGER, JR., AND SEAN WILENTZ

GENERAL EDITORS

Times Books

HENRY HOLT AND COMPANY   NEW YORK

Times Books
Henry Holt and Company, LLC
Publishers since 1866
175 Fifth Avenue
New York, New York 10010
www.henryholt.com

Copyright © 2017 by Michael Tomasky
All rights reserved.
Distributed in Canada by Raincoast Book Distribution Limited

Frontispiece: J. DAVID AKE/AFP/Getty Images

Library of Congress Cataloging-in-Publication Data

Names: Tomasky, Michael, 1960– author.
Title: Bill Clinton : the 42nd president, 1993–2001 / Michael Tomasky.
Description: New York : Times Books, 2017. | Series: The American presidents
series | Includes bibliographical references and index.
Identifiers: LCCN 2016024648| ISBN 9781627796767 (hardcover) | ISBN
9781627796774 (electronic book)
Subjects: LCSH: Clinton, Bill, 1946– | Presidents—United States—Biography.
| United States—Politics and government—1993–2001.
Classification: LCC E886 .T66 2017 | DDC 973.929092 [B] —dc23
LC record available at https://lccn.loc.gov/2016024648

Our books may be purchased in bulk for promotional, educational, or business use.
Please contact your local bookseller or the Macmillan Corporate and Premium Sales
Department at (800) 221-7945, extension 5442, or by e-mail at MacmillanSpecial
Markets@macmillan.com.

First Edition 2017

Printed in the United States of America

1 3 5 7 9 10 8 6 4 2

To Margot

Contents

Editor's Note

THE AMERICAN PRESIDENCY

The president is the central player in the American political order. That would seem to contradict the intentions of the Founding Fathers. Remembering the horrid example of the British monarchy, they invented a separation of powers in order, as Justice Brandeis later put it, "to preclude the exercise of arbitrary power." Accordingly, they divided the government into three allegedly equal and coordinate branches—the executive, the legislative, and the judiciary.

But a system based on the tripartite separation of powers has an inherent tendency toward inertia and stalemate. One of the three branches must take the initiative if the system is to move. The executive branch alone is structurally capable of taking that initiative. The Founders must have sensed this when they accepted Alexander Hamilton's proposition in the Seventieth Federalist that "energy in the executive is a leading character in the definition of good government." They thus envisaged a strong president—but within an equally strong system of constitutional accountability. (The term *imperial presidency* arose in the 1970s to describe the situation when the balance between power and accountability is upset in favor of the executive.)

The American system of self-government thus comes to focus

in the presidency—"the vital place of action in the system," as Woodrow Wilson put it. Henry Adams, himself the great-grandson and grandson of presidents as well as the most brilliant of American historians, said that the American president "resembles the commander of a ship at sea. He must have a helm to grasp, a course to steer, a port to seek." The men in the White House (thus far only men, alas) in steering their chosen courses have shaped our destiny as a nation.

Biography offers an easy education in American history, rendering the past more human, more vivid, more intimate, more accessible, more connected to ourselves. Biography reminds us that presidents are not supermen. They are human beings too, worrying about decisions, attending to wives and children, juggling balls in the air, and putting on their pants one leg at a time. Indeed, as Emerson contended, "There is properly no history; only biography."

Presidents serve us as inspirations, and they also serve us as warnings. They provide bad examples as well as good. The nation, the Supreme Court has said, has "no right to expect that it will always have wise and humane rulers, sincerely attached to the principles of the Constitution. Wicked men, ambitious of power, with hatred of liberty and contempt of law, may fill the place once occupied by Washington and Lincoln."

The men in the White House express the ideals and the values, the frailties and the flaws, of the voters who send them there. It is altogether natural that we should want to know more about the virtues and the vices of the fellows we have elected to govern us. As we know more about them, we will know more about ourselves. The French political philosopher Joseph de Maistre said, "Every nation has the government it deserves."

At the start of the twenty-first century, forty-two men have made it to the Oval Office. (George W. Bush is counted our forty-third president, because Grover Cleveland, who served nonconsecutive terms, is counted twice.) Of the parade of presidents, a dozen or so lead the polls periodically conducted by historians and political scientists. What makes a great president?

Great presidents possess, or are possessed by, a vision of an ideal America. Their passion, as they grasp the helm, is to set the ship of state on the right course toward the port they seek. Great presidents also have a deep psychic connection with the needs, anxieties, dreams of people. "I do not believe," said Wilson, "that any man can lead who does not act . . . under the impulse of a profound sympathy with those whom he leads—a sympathy which is insight—an insight which is of the heart rather than of the intellect."

"All of our great presidents," said Franklin D. Roosevelt, "were leaders of thought at a time when certain ideas in the life of the nation had to be clarified." So Washington incarnated the idea of federal union, Jefferson and Jackson the idea of democracy, Lincoln union and freedom, Cleveland rugged honesty. Theodore Roosevelt and Wilson, said FDR, were both "moral leaders, each in his own way and his own time, who used the presidency as a pulpit."

To succeed, presidents not only must have a port to seek but they must convince Congress and the electorate that it is a port worth seeking. Politics in a democracy is ultimately an educational process, an adventure in persuasion and consent. Every president stands in Theodore Roosevelt's bully pulpit.

The greatest presidents in the scholars' rankings, Washington, Lincoln, and Franklin Roosevelt, were leaders who confronted and overcame the republic's greatest crises. Crisis widens presidential opportunities for bold and imaginative action. But it does not guarantee presidential greatness. The crisis of secession did not spur Buchanan or the crisis of depression spur Hoover to creative leadership. Their inadequacies in the face of crisis allowed Lincoln and the second Roosevelt to show the difference individuals make to history. Still, even in the absence of first-order crisis, forceful and persuasive presidents—Jefferson, Jackson, James K. Polk, Theodore Roosevelt, Harry Truman, John F. Kennedy, Ronald Reagan, George W. Bush— are able to impose their own priorities on the country.

The diverse drama of the presidency offers a fascinating set of tales. Biographies of American presidents constitute a chronicle of wisdom and folly, nobility and pettiness, courage and cunning, forthrightness and deceit, quarrel and consensus. The turmoil perennially swirling around the White House illuminates the heart of the American democracy.

It is the aim of the American Presidents series to present the grand panorama of our chief executives in volumes compact enough for the busy reader, lucid enough for the student, authoritative enough for the scholar. Each volume offers a distillation of character and career. I hope that these lives will give readers some understanding of the pitfalls and potentialities of the presidency and also of the responsibilities of citizenship. Truman's famous sign—"The buck stops here"—tells only half the story. Citizens cannot escape the ultimate responsibility. It is in the voting booth, not on the presidential desk, that the buck finally stops.

—Arthur M. Schlesinger, Jr.

Bill Clinton

1

A Young Fellow in a Hurry

It was the summer after Bill Clinton finished first grade. Roger Clinton, the man Bill grew up calling "Daddy" even though he was not Bill's biological father, had grown tired of Hope, Arkansas, and its comparative lack of amusements, so he moved the family to Hot Springs—a town much more up his hooch-hitting, hard-living alley. Roger bought a farm, and one Sunday, Bill was out playing with his cousin Karla when the farm's one mean ram began to charge at them. Karla, older and faster, got away. Bill tripped over a rock. As he tells the story in his autobiography, *My Life*:

> Soon he caught me and knocked my legs out from under me. Before I could get up he butted me in the head. Then I was stunned and hurt and couldn't get up. So he backed up, got a good head start, and rammed me again as hard as he could. He did the same thing over and over and over again, alternating his targets between my head and my gut. Soon I was pouring blood and hurting like the devil.

In due course Uncle Raymond, Karla's father, smote the beast between the eyes with a rock, and it backed off. Bill's injuries were surprisingly few—just a scar on his forehead. But he learned that "I could take a hard hit."

He must have thought about that ram more than once when he was in the White House. Clinton's was a presidency of many notable accomplishments, especially with regard to the economy. But easily his most notable accomplishment was simply surviving—and, just as with that ram, often emerging with surprisingly few injuries. Clinton's rise to national prominence coincided with the ascent of what his friend and adviser Sidney Blumenthal had labeled, in a widely influential book published in 1986, the conservative "counter-establishment." But not even Blumenthal could have predicted how hopped up that counter-establishment would be by 1992. For the ensuing eight years, it would hit Clinton with everything it had—although sometimes he helped its cause with his own poor judgment.

Through it all, from the various campaign controversies to the Whitewater allegations to the Lewinsky indignity—prominent television newsman Sam Donaldson told viewers just after the Lewinsky story broke that Clinton's presidency "could be numbered in *days*"—Bill Clinton survived and even triumphed. He left an enviable record of achievements, helped guide the country into the new Information Age, and after a shaky start developed into a respected global leader. Fifteen years after he left office, Clinton consistently ranked as America's most popular recent ex-president, and he'd jumped up several notches in the historical assessments of political scientists. At the same time, during the 2016 Democratic presidential primary, some of his accomplishments underwent a withering reexamination by a younger and more liberal generation of voters for whom Clinton's compromises on crime, welfare, and other matters were anathema. And the media persisted in its general posture of deep suspicion of both Clintons. So Bill Clinton still often found himself in survival mode, deflecting (not always artfully) various accusations and insinuations about the Clinton Foundation, his public speaking fees, or his record on crime. At either end of the political spectrum, and inside a political press often driven by scandal and pseudo-scandal mongering, Clinton could not completely shed the label—first affixed to him by right-wing Arkansas opinion columnists back in the early 1980s—of "Slick Willie."

Back as far as his boyhood, Clinton lived on the edge. In 1992, his presidential campaign offered up some syrupy bio ads about "The Man from Hope." What campaign publicist could resist such a fortuity? But in truth, Clinton spent most of his formative years, from age six onward, in the saucier town of Hot Springs. He was born William Jefferson Blythe III on August 19, 1946, but his father, William Jefferson Blythe Jr., died before he was born. He was raised by his mother, Virginia, and, even more, by her parents, while she was in New Orleans pursuing her education. Virginia met and married Roger Clinton, a car salesman, and it wasn't long before Roger pined to return with his new family (which soon included another son, Roger Jr.) to his hometown.

That's the milieu that largely formed Bill Clinton—Virginia, a hardworking nurse-anesthetist but also a salty good timer whom he utterly adored; Roger, his basically decent but alcoholic and sometimes violent stepfather; a raucous cavalcade of aunts and uncles, the women bearing names such as Otie and Ilaree and Falba; the Hot Springs thoroughbred racing track, to which his mother was no stranger; the town's gambling parlors and whorehouses and bail bondsman storefronts, giving the place the feel of Frank Capra's dystopian vision of post–Bedford Falls Pottersville in *It's a Wonderful Life*; even the presence of the famed New York mobster Owney Madden, who had "retired" to Hot Springs and lived as a quasi-respectable senior citizen, and whom Virginia Clinton once put under anesthetic.

As a teenager Clinton was chubby, as he acknowledges at several points in *My Life*. But he loved people, their stories, their company. He was smart, and he got As in school—except in citizenship, because he couldn't stop talking in class. He marched in the band, but he also put his excellent saxophone skills to more sophisticated—and, to girls, alluring—use by playing in the high school jazz ensemble. Famously, he went to Washington, D.C., once as part of a Boys Nation trip and shook the hand of President John F. Kennedy. By his senior year, writes his biographer David Maraniss, "everything in the house revolved around the golden son." He knew from about age sixteen that his vocation would be politics: "I loved music and thought I could be very good, but I knew I would never be John Coltrane or Stan Getz. I was interested in medicine and thought I could be a fine doctor, but I knew I would never be Michael DeBakey. But I knew I could be great in public service."

And soon it was time to get out of Arkansas and study it all close-up. So in the fall of 1964, off he went to Washington and to Georgetown University.

· · ·

The Georgetown of that time was divided into two campuses—the Yard, the main campus, which was male and home mostly to Catholic boys from the Northeast; and the East Campus, which had the Edmund A. Walsh School of Foreign Service and a few other divisions, and a more diverse student body. Clinton was in the Foreign Service school and, being one of the few Southern Baptists around, added to the diversity. He won the class presidency in his sophomore and junior years, and landed a part-time job in the office of the legendary Arkansas senator J. William Fulbright, who was chairman of the Senate Foreign Relations Committee during this time, when American involvement in the Vietnam War was escalating. Clinton performed the types of menial tasks young aides still perform today, which in his case included delivering to Fulbright—and sometimes reading—confidential governmental memoranda about the war, which showed how badly it was going. Every day, Fulbright received a list of the names of Arkansas boys who'd died in Vietnam. One day Clinton looked down at the list and saw a good friend's name. He was so overcome with grief and guilt, he writes in *My Life*, that "I briefly flirted with the idea of dropping out of school and enlisting in the military—after all, I was a democrat in philosophy as well as party; I didn't feel entitled to escape even a war I had come to oppose."

That is not the path Clinton took. During his senior year at

Georgetown, he applied for and won a Rhodes scholarship to study at Oxford University after his graduation. And so in the late summer of 1968, Bill Clinton from Hot Springs, Arkansas, was on his way to England. He would "read" politics, philosophy, and economics at Oxford, and during his two years there would visit several world capitals; he even traveled to the Soviet Union to see what life was like behind the Iron Curtain.

But the draft was always looming for young men of Clinton's generation. During his time at Georgetown and Oxford, Clinton pursued avenues to avoid active duty in combat. He first tried and failed to win navy and air force commissions that would have ensured he wouldn't be a frontline soldier. But the crucial events took place in the summer and fall of 1969, after his first year in England. Clinton told Colonel Eugene Holmes, the commander of the Army Reserve Officers' Training Corps at the University of Arkansas, that he would attend law school that fall in Fayetteville and join the ROTC. But Clinton didn't follow through on that promise and instead went back to Oxford. He writes in *My Life* that the delay was a function of ROTC rules, under which he couldn't be formally enrolled until the following summer. Then, on December 1, he drew a high draft lottery number and was effectively in the clear. It was only then that he wrote to Holmes saying that he wouldn't be attending Arkansas after all and thanking him for "saving me from the draft."

In retrospect, there seems little chance that a graduate of Georgetown and a Rhodes scholar would have been placed on the front lines—surely the army would have valued him more for his brains than his brawn. Besides, for someone who wanted to be in politics, what could look better on the résumé than that he took his chances and served his country, even during a war he opposed? But there was no way of knowing these things at the time. Clinton opposed the war viscerally and wasn't driven wholly by calculation, but at the same time it seems clear that it wasn't principle alone that motivated him.

Anyway, he got out of it.

In May 1970, the time of the Kent State shootings, Clinton was finishing his second and final year at Oxford and learned that he had been accepted at Yale Law School. Like all Ivy League law classes, Clinton's included a number of matriculants who would go on to join the elite—Richard Blumenthal, who would become a U.S. senator from Connecticut; a number of future members of Congress, federal judges, diplomats, and university presidents; and Robert Reich, who had been one of Clinton's fellow Rhodes scholars and would later serve as secretary of labor in his administration.

But there was one student in particular whose presence would change Clinton's life, and he hers. He described first laying eyes on Hillary Diane Rodham thus:

> Then one day, when I was sitting in the back of Professor Emerson's class in Political and Civil Rights, I spotted a woman I hadn't seen before. Apparently she attended even less frequently than I did. She had thick dark blond hair and wore eyeglasses and no makeup, but she conveyed a sense of strength and self-possession I had rarely seen in anyone, man or woman.

They were, by all accounts, inseparable from that point on, even if, as we know, he sometimes separated himself into the embrace of other women. They spent the summer following their second year of law school in Texas, helping coordinate the statewide efforts of Senator George McGovern's 1972 presidential campaign, where Bill worked alongside a young television director named Steven Spielberg. The following year, with their law degrees secured, Hillary headed to Washington to join the staff of the House Judiciary Committee during the height of the Watergate scandal, and Bill moved back to Arkansas to teach law and pursue a political career. In biographies of Hillary, this is inevitably adjudged the fateful moment: when, after President Richard Nixon's resignation in August 1974, she decided not to stay in Washington or move to New York, where a limitless future awaited her, but to go down to a hayseed state and subordinate her ambitions to a man's. It's a story that has been elaborately, and inaccurately, adorned over the years. They married on October 11, 1975.

Bill Clinton ran for Congress in 1974, the year of the Democrats' most overwhelming electoral triumph in the past half century, immediately in the wake of Watergate and Nixon's resignation. It was an uphill race against an entrenched Republican incumbent, John Paul Hammerschmidt. In that year of the "Watergate babies," when so many young Democrats won election to the House and Senate, Clinton didn't quite make it to the mountaintop; he got 48 percent. But even while losing that race, he left a footprint. "He showed up at the Pope County picnic in 1974—which is our traditional political kickoff—opened his mouth, and everyone just knew," said George Jernigan, an Arkansas politician.

Two years later, Clinton set his sights on the office of Arkansas attorney general, where he faced Jernigan and one other opponent in the Democratic primary (oddly, no Republican ran). As Jernigan would succinctly recall, "He beat the living hell out of me." In the South especially, where regulations are few and state legislatures tend not to be energetic with respect to their investigatory powers, a state attorney general can make a good name for himself by taking on a well-chosen powerful interest. Clinton chose very well indeed: he battled Arkansas Power and Light, opposing a rate increase and an attempt to build a costly coal-fired power plant in the state.

The profile he gained in that office positioned him well to run for governor in 1978. He breezed past four opponents in the Democratic primary and swamped his Republican foe, becoming at age thirty-two the nation's youngest governor.

• • •

He was a young fellow in a hurry, and by all accounts too much of a hurry. He was credited in that first term with doing good work on education, getting the legislature to raise teachers' salaries. His other big goal was transportation and road improvement. He

proposed increasing the car tag levy, and he wanted to do it by
the value of the car, so that Arkansans driving old pickup trucks
would take less of a hit than those tooling around in new Lincolns.
But the state legislature approved an increase based on vehicle
weight, which hit working people harder. The young governor had
a choice: sign a bill that accomplished his goal but in what he considered to be a bad way, or have no bill at all. He signed. "It was
the single dumbest mistake I ever made in politics until 1994," he
writes in *My Life*, referring to the year of his fateful decision to
agree to the appointment of a Whitewater special prosecutor.

Then, in Clinton's reelection year of 1980 (gubernatorial terms
in Arkansas were then just two years), Fidel Castro deported
120,000 political prisoners and "undesirables," who sailed to Florida for refuge. President Jimmy Carter, facing reelection that
year, had a huge crisis on his hands, which he had to deal with by
locating these people in various federal facilities, one of which was
Fort Chaffee in Arkansas. On the night of June 1, about a thousand of them broke out. The National Guard defied Clinton's
instructions to block the Cubans from getting anywhere that might
bring them into contact with Arkansans, who, Clinton knew, would
be worked up—and armed. No one died that night, but sixty-two
people were injured before order was restored.

Car tags and Cubans were the main reasons Clinton was defeated
for reelection in 1980—the last election he ever lost. There were
others. An ancillary one revolved around the birth of his daughter,
Chelsea, in February of that year. This man who'd never known
his biological father wanted to make sure that his child knew hers,
and some say he lost a little focus then. But mainly the explana-
tions are centered on the widely shared impression that he was a
know-it-all who had stopped listening to people.

The loss devastated him. He thought his political career was
over, and he nearly ended it of his own volition—he seriously considered multiple job offers, from heading the World Wildlife Fund
to becoming the president of the University of Louisville. But in
the end he stayed in Little Rock and joined a law firm. Then one

day in the spring of 1981, at a small-town gas station, he ran into a man whose rage at that car tag increase was so thoroughgoing that he bragged to the ex-governor that he'd persuaded ten family members to vote against him. Clinton then asked the man if he'd consider voting for him if he ran again. The man said, "Sure I would. We're even now." Clinton ran to a pay phone, called Hillary, and told her he thought he could regain the governorship in 1982.

Here, Dick Morris enters the picture for the first time. Clinton brought in Morris, a New York political consultant, to advise him on his comeback. Morris worked with Tony Schwartz, the adman who had made the famous Goldwater-daisy-nuclear-countdown commercial for Lyndon Johnson in 1964, to create a mea culpa ad starring Clinton to launch his 1982 campaign. "My daddy never had to whip me twice for the same thing," the once and future governor said. Meanwhile, another quasi-apology: Hillary announced that she would henceforth be known not as Hillary Rodham but as Hillary Rodham Clinton, finally bowing to custom and taking her husband's name. Bill Clinton went around the state talking about the lessons of defeat, and he won over the voters who had thrown him out two years earlier. It also helped that the state's economy wasn't in great shape, and come election night Clinton won 55 percent of the vote.

Back in office, Clinton now set his sights higher. He began an aggressive effort to transform his state, in an attempt to receive some national notice. The biggest marker here was a package of education reforms, an effort that he appointed Hillary to lead. The state greatly increased its investments in education; more controversially, the package included a teacher testing program that infuriated the Arkansas Education Association, and Governor Clinton and the union's president had numerous debates about it that sometimes drew national attention. He also raised the sales tax to help fund Arkansas's schools, after the state Supreme Court ruled that the state's school financing system was inequitable and unconstitutional. Results in the classroom were positive if short of overwhelming; graduation rates rose and many more high schools began to offer advanced science classes, in some cases where they hadn't taught chemistry at all.

Arkansas has never been known as a laboratory for cutting-edge progressive change. Its political culture has historically been dominated by big industries such as oil and gas, poultry, and lumber— and, by Clinton's time, the Walton family, whose Wal-Mart stores started in Bentonville. Clinton certainly made his peace with these interests, but he did change the political culture of the state to a considerable extent. He expanded access to health care for poor children. His economic development and job-training efforts helped buffer the state against the worst effects of two recessions. He fought the old-line segregationists, led by the notorious "Justice Jim" Johnson, an associate justice on the state supreme court, and pushed hard for the integration of the state's schools and workplaces. (Clinton always wore their enmity as a particular point of pride.) And he developed a reputation as an innovator at a time when many Democrats were talking about "reinventing government" as a way of pushing back against the prevailing anti-government sentiment of the Reagan years.

Meanwhile, the Democratic Party nationally was in its worst shape since the 1920s. In the 1984 presidential election, Ronald Reagan destroyed Walter Mondale, who carried only his home state of Minnesota and the District of Columbia. The postelection conventional wisdom held that the party had become reflexively paleo-liberal, chained to its special interests. If it didn't modernize, it might never win the White House again. An Indiana native named Al From, who'd worked on the Johnson-era War on Poverty and in the Carter White House, took it upon himself in 1985 to create the vehicle that would remake the Democratic Party: the Democratic Leadership Council (DLC). Clinton was involved from the start, invoked by the group as a model for the type of "New Democrat" who could make the party competitive again in national elections.

Clinton kept at his job, winning reelection every two years and shifting his emphasis toward the state's economic development. Hillary settled in to her work at the Rose Law Firm, one of Little

Rock's largest and most influential firms. The Clintons were not among Arkansas's richest citizens; he barely made $35,000 as governor, and she usually brought home around $100,000, which was a very nice living in Little Rock, but not all that much for a law partner in a major firm. In 1986, in an effort to build up their personal wealth, they invested in a land-development deal in the Ozarks called Whitewater. They entered into the arrangement with Jim McDougal, a friend and political science professor, but in the end the investment didn't pan out—they lost around $50,000 on the deal and had good reason to think that that was the end of it.

No particular aura of scandal surrounded Arkansas's first couple. There was the sense that he was overly clever and calculating (the "Slick Willie" business). There was gossip about Bill's extramarital excursions, presumed to be numerous, and he aroused the kinds of passionate emotional responses in supporters and (especially) detractors that one would expect of a brash, young governor trying to alter a sedentary political culture, but few thought him genuinely corrupt.

. . .

By 1988, Clinton was running for his fifth term and was enough of a national figure that he was given a coveted slot at that year's Democratic convention: placing Governor Michael Dukakis's name in nomination. He was supposed to talk for fifteen minutes. The convention delegates, who started chanting "We Want Duke!" just six minutes into Clinton's speech, were first bewildered and then exasperated and finally infuriated—and booing loudly—as Clinton just wouldn't stop talking, insouciantly smiling through the catcalls. When he finally finished, thirty-three minutes had elapsed. At least he was talking about Dukakis and not himself, but it was impossible to imagine what he was thinking—his first national exposure, and he turned himself into a punch line. It did, however, land him a guest spot on *The Tonight Show* soon thereafter, and he was appropriately self-effacing as Johnny Carson needled him.

Dukakis's loss was the Democrats' third straight, and now From, who felt that the DLC had failed to have sufficient influence on Dukakis's platform, saw his opening. Clinton was the horse From hoped to ride to the White House. From had met Clinton in 1979 or 1980, he says, but started to get to know him well in 1987, soon after Clinton had impressed From with a speech he gave at a DLC meeting. Over the course of 1987 and 1988, From says, the two spoke constantly, and From quickly became persuaded that Clinton could carry the New Democrats' message to victory. From was also impressed by Clinton's recall, his attention to detail, and his exuberance with people. And so he made his pitch. As he later recalled:

> A little after four o'clock on the afternoon of April 6, 1989, I walked into the office of Governor Bill Clinton on the second floor of the Arkansas State Capitol in Little Rock.
>
> "I've got a deal for you," I told Clinton after a few minutes of political chitchat. "If you agree to become chairman of the DLC, we'll pay for your travel around the country, we'll work together on an agenda, and I think you'll be president one day and we'll both be important." With that proposition, Clinton agreed to become chairman of the Democratic Leadership Council, and our partnership was born.

From soon saw for himself that he'd made the right choice. After Clinton became the DLC chair, he and From traveled to about twenty-five states together. "We'd leave from Little Rock or maybe Washington," From recalled, "and we'd travel the whole day and get to San Francisco at eleven o'clock at night, and he'd see somebody in the lobby and he'd go, 'Oh, I remember you. You did this and this and this when I first ran for Congress in 1974.' It was just out of sight."

From's strategy was broader than just finding the right candidate. It involved intellectual spadework, which in 1989 produced one of the most famous white papers in white-paper history: "The Politics of Evasion," by the scholars and party activists William A.

Galston and Elaine C. Kamarck. It argued that "too many Americans have come to see the [Democratic] party as inattentive to their economic interests, indifferent if not hostile to their moral sentiments, and ineffective in defense of their national security," and laid the groundwork for a DLC platform that departed from liberal orthodoxy in all three realms. As Kenneth S. Baer, who participated in and chronicled the rise of the New Democrat movement, has noted:

> Throughout 1990 and 1991, the DLC plied [Clinton] with critical aid during this important "invisible primary" phase of the campaign. The organization unveiled a developed and distinct public philosophy that took controversial stands on a variety of issues, and it established state chapters to give its putative candidate a reason to travel the country and a chance to construct a network of supporters in key states.

Most of the national media, and many Democrats, were waiting to see what New York governor Mario Cuomo was going to do. Though he was more of a traditional Democrat, he was considered in the fall of 1991 the strong favorite for the Democratic nomination—he was the governor of a large and important state, and he had won liberal hearts and minds with a galvanizing speech at the party's 1984 convention. The thinking among the experts was that if Cuomo ran, he filled the "governor slot" and there was no room for Clinton. But Clinton saw matters differently.

2

The Comeback Kid

In October 1991, President George H. W. Bush was sitting on an intimidating Gallup approval rating of 64 percent. More than that, it seemed to many political observers that the White House simply "belonged" to the Republican Party. In 1988, Bush had clobbered Michael Dukakis, 426 electoral votes to just 111. Bush won a number of large-population states that in only a few years would come to be thought of as solidly Democratic: California, Illinois, Pennsylvania, Michigan, New Jersey, and Maryland. But no one could have seen that then. At the time, the Democratic Party had the three major problems that Galston and Kamarck described in their paper: it was not trusted on issues relating to the economy and the role of government, considered out of the mainstream on social issues, and labeled "soft" on national security. The job of turning those perceptions around and taking back the White House looked like an awfully heavy lift.

Of the Democrats lining up to take a shot at it, aside from Cuomo, Senator Bob Kerrey of Nebraska seemed best on paper. Not only was he a senator, but he had previously served as Nebraska's governor, so he had proved he could win in a Republican state. Kerrey had served in Vietnam as well. Senator Tom Harkin of Iowa was a native of the state that hosted the first caucuses and had close ties to organized labor. Former senator Paul Tsongas of Massachusetts cared most about reducing the deficit, and thus could stand immune from any charge of being an old-line liberal. Douglas Wilder was the first African American governor of Virginia. And Jerry Brown was a former governor of California who was positioning himself as a populist, refusing campaign contributions greater than $100 and attracting appreciative laughter (from supporters) and cynical snickers (from detractors) as he stood at podiums in those pre-Internet days and recited the toll-free number that his hoped-for army of small donors could call.

Excitement about Clinton—among New Democrats, if not old ones—had been building since May 1991, when he gave an inspiring speech at a DLC convention in Cleveland. It was there that he first articulated the three-word mantra of "opportunity, responsibility, and community" that would define the New Democrat approach. Each word was intended to carry a message for the swing voters who had abandoned the party in the prior three elections. *Opportunity* was meant to convey that the Democrats were now pro-growth and not concerned only with economic fairness and equality; *responsibility* was aimed at fighting the widely held perception that the party gave too many handouts to those who didn't work (and carried a strong racial subtext); and *community* was intended to suggest that New Democrats wouldn't ignore broader community goals and standards in favor of individual or group claims that seemed outside the cultural mainstream. "We have got to have a message that touches everybody, that makes sense to everybody, that goes beyond the stale orthodoxies of left and right, one that resonates with the real concerns of ordinary Americans, with their hopes and their fears," Clinton said.

He was still governor, and he had promised his state's voters in 1990 that he would serve a full term, which was now four years. He drove around the state in the spring of 1991 asking voters' permission to go back on that promise, and he generally received it. At a July 4 picnic, he saw the first "Clinton for President" signs. By the time he celebrated his forty-fifth birthday on August 19, he had started assembling his team—Stan Greenberg to do polling, Frank

Greer to make ads, and Mandy Grunwald to plan the broader communications strategy. And on October 3, at the Little Rock statehouse, Clinton made his candidacy official. "A Clinton administration," he promised, "won't spend our money on programs that don't solve problems and a government that doesn't work. I want to reinvent government to make it more efficient and more effective. I want to give citizens more choices in the services they get, and empower them to make those choices."

On December 15, 1991, Clinton decisively won a nonbinding straw poll in Florida. It was an early sign of organizational strength in a key state, although, as the *New York Times* noted at the time, "Mr. Clinton's opponents said that given the attention he focused on the straw poll, he was the only candidate who had any real stake in its outcome." And then, on December 20, Mario Cuomo announced that he would not run. He was set to fly to New Hampshire to file his papers of candidacy for that state's primary, and he had even instructed the gubernatorial airplane to rev its engines. But at the last minute he left the airplane sitting on an Albany tarmac. The presumed front-runner was out. The thing was wide open.

Because Harkin was from Iowa, his competitors barely contested the caucuses that year, and Harkin got 77 percent of the vote. Even in New Hampshire, there was a near-favorite son: Tsongas lived in Lowell, Massachusetts, very close to the New Hampshire border. So it was assumed that he would probably win. The battle was to see who finished second, and how close that candidate could come. In mid-January, Clinton was well positioned. And then came the two controversies that would define the campaign. The month would be Clinton's fire walk.

. . .

On January 23, 1992, the political world got word that a supermarket tabloid, the *Star*, was in possession of transcripts of telephone conversations Clinton had had with an alleged ex-paramour named Gennifer Flowers, a TV reporter and Little Rock chanteuse.

The media in the state capital, the journalists who'd covered Clinton for years and the few national reporters who happened to be there, lit into a frenzy. Clinton was flying back home that day for another reason: he was coming to sign the execution order of Ricky Ray Rector, a convicted and brain-damaged cop killer. This was a time of high crime rates, and the move was another signal to centrist voters that Clinton was a different kind of Democrat—tough on crime and not a softhearted liberal. (Rector was so mentally incompetent that after his last meal he left his dessert in his cell as he was hauled off to meet his fate because he wanted to save it for later.)

Clinton's roving eye had been the subject of much gossip for some time by then. The previous presidential campaign was the first in which a candidate (Gary Hart) had been asked by the media about marital infidelity, and journalists went so far as to stake out the Washington apartment of Hart's girlfriend. But even that episode didn't compare to this. Clinton generated far more intense passions within his party, pro and con, than Hart had. And since Hart had been forced to withdraw, and there was no precedent for a major politician surviving such a revelation, everyone wondered: was the Democrats' seeming best hope for victory going to be knocked out of the race before it started?

For a few days the campaign flailed. Then *60 Minutes* invited Bill and Hillary Clinton to be interviewed on Sunday, January 26, 1992, which would mean they'd be on the air right after CBS's broadcast of the Super Bowl. The interview, by Steve Kroft, was taped that morning in a Boston hotel room. The only thing Clinton explicitly denied was the charge that he'd had a "twelve-year affair" with Flowers. He acknowledged causing "pain" in his marriage. At one point, Kroft referred to the Clintons' union as an "arrangement," and here, Clinton interrupted and played a little offense: "Wait a minute. You're looking at two people who love each other. This is not an arrangement or an understanding. This is a marriage."

It was enough. Polls showed that people understood what

Clinton was saying, and the Flowers story wasn't going to finish him off. But just as all that was dying down, on February 6, the *Wall Street Journal* broke the story of Clinton's efforts to avoid the draft in 1969. Colonel Holmes, who throughout Clinton's political career in Arkansas had said that he'd handled Clinton's case the same as anyone else's, now told the *Journal*'s Jeffrey Birnbaum that he felt Clinton had duped him—that Clinton's verbal commitment to ROTC was just a way to get out of serving. (Holmes was a World War II veteran who had been held as a prisoner of war in the Philippines and forced into the Bataan Death March.) A few days later, ABC made public a letter that Clinton had written to Holmes that included the sentence "I decided to accept the draft in spite of my beliefs for one reason: to maintain my political viability within the system."

One of Clinton's top campaign advisers, James Carville, argued in internal discussions that "this letter is our friend," and indeed it included its share of thoughtful passages. But all anyone ever mentioned was "political viability." The campaign was in a panic. Pollster Stan Greenberg recalls that he could see Clinton's numbers dropping, as Clinton himself later put it, like "a turd in a well." There was a conference call on which the pollster delivered the bad news. "I can't remember if I used the word *meltdown*," he says, "but the numbers just went off a cliff." There was talk of withdrawing, but Clinton wasn't having that, and instead the campaign shifted into high gear. Clinton campaigned almost nonstop, arguing to people that their votes should be about the future, not something that had happened more than twenty years earlier.

When the votes were counted, Clinton finished second in New Hampshire, with 25 percent to Tsongas's 33 percent. It wasn't a win, but it was enough for the campaign to spin Clinton as "the Comeback Kid," and an obliging media, for whom Clinton provided what was clearly the best story line among the Democrats, bought it. What turned things around? Somewhere in the twelve days between when the draft story broke and when the voting took place, the voters seemed to have turned some kind of psychological corner. In his book *All Too Human*, campaign aide George Stephanopoulos reflects:

> What I didn't realize at the time was how the focus on Clinton's problems was paradoxically helping him, turning the New Hampshire primary into a referendum on what politics should be about. Clinton was channeling public disgust and transforming it into a reason to vote for him. The best way to strike a blow against the obsession with scandal was to vote for the candidate most plagued by scandal.

From that point on, Clinton was more or less immunized against scandal. He rolled through the primaries, sweeping the South. He hit a late pothole when Jerry Brown upset him in Connecticut, which lent some drama to the New York primary—it seemed briefly that perhaps Brown could win the Empire State. But Clinton had won the Illinois and Michigan primaries three weeks prior, on March 17, 1992, and it was clear from then that he was going to collect enough delegates to be the nominee.

The period between the end of the primary season and the beginning of the general election battle is often an awkward one for campaigns. For the Clinton team, it was something worse than that. The main reason was the appearance of H. Ross Perot, the Dallas businessman who'd made his fortune in federal data systems contracting and who had become a public figure largely through his pronouncements on the evils of the federal deficit. For some years, political scientists had forecast the emergence of a "radical center" in American politics—voters who hated both parties and wanted sweeping change but not in a uniformly left or right direction. "Irresponsible" federal spending was exactly the kind of issue that infuriated such voters.

Perot was radical centrism personified, and he lit a fire across the heartland. In June, he led both Clinton and Bush in the polls. Clinton was exhausted and overweight. And worst of all, recalled

Greenberg, "In our own polls we were in third place. There were people who were talking about not going to the convention. And we were just above the threshold for public funding. It was pretty tough. And he was depressed."

Late June brought a moment that has lived in history in some ways more than any other in the campaign. Jesse Jackson's Rainbow PUSH Coalition was meeting at a Washington hotel. Several hundred attendees—mostly African American educators, labor leaders, and activists—spent three days listening to speakers such as the financier Felix Rohatyn, who came to talk about infrastructure investment. Clinton was due to address the gathering on its last day. This was originally supposed to be a bridge-building event between the New Democrat candidate and the civil rights leader who had twice sought the Democratic nomination, in 1984 and 1988. Jackson was the moral leader of the left wing of the Democratic Party, which regarded the Democratic Leadership Council as too willing to sell out the party's principles. Jackson had memorably called the DLC "Democrats of the Leisure Class."

But the night before Clinton's speech, a little-known rapper named Sister Souljah spoke at a panel on youth. Some weeks prior, during the riots in Los Angeles that followed the acquittal of the police officers who had beaten Rodney King, she had given an interview in which she said blacks should stop killing one another and have a week when they killed whites. Clinton writes in *My Life* that he had thought of denouncing her at the time but refrained because the circumstances didn't feel right to him. (He was in Los Angeles at a charity event.) But now, with Clinton appearing at the same venue as Souljah, he agreed with those aides who pushed him to use the moment as a way to distance himself from the liberal (and black) Jackson wing of the party and send the message to centrist white voters that he wouldn't kowtow to "them."

Clinton rebuked Souljah, saying that if you took her use of the words *white* and *black* and reversed them, "you might think David Duke was giving that speech." It got Clinton some great press: Democrat stands up to mau-mauing interest group! Presidential candidates ever since have kept an alert eye open for just the right kind of interest-group punching bag that would permit them a potential "Sister Souljah moment."

. . .

The next month, in July, the campaign's fortunes grew even better. First, on July 9, Clinton chose Senator Albert Gore Jr. of Tennessee to be his running mate, in defiance of the convention that a running mate should be from a different wing of the party and a different region of the country—and, in the forty-five-year-old Clinton's case, should have been an older, experienced Washington hand, preferably with some foreign policy experience. Gore had some of that—up to this point, he had mostly distinguished himself in Congress as a rare Democratic expert on weapons systems and the nuclear arsenal. But in the main Gore was much more like Clinton than unlike him: a southerner, a New Democrat, and a baby boomer. Indeed, the chief message Clinton wanted to send was one of generational change: Gore was a year and a half younger than Clinton, so the duo, if they won, would be the youngest ticket ever elected in the country's history.

Four days later, the Democrats opened their convention at New York's Madison Square Garden. The party was still known for chaotic conventions in this era, whereas the Republicans had already mastered the art of turning them into slick and airless coronations. In 1972, just twenty years earlier, the party's nominee, George McGovern, hadn't been able to deliver his acceptance speech until three a.m., owing to an undisciplined and drawn-out vice presidential nominating process in which delegates barked out such names as Archie Bunker and Martha Mitchell. In 1980, the tensions between the Jimmy Carter and Ted Kennedy camps had been palpable.

There were a few rough edges at the 1992 convention: Governor Bob Casey of Pennsylvania, who opposed abortion rights, was denied a speaking slot. Jerry Brown, who had still not withdrawn from the race, seconded his own nomination. But in essence the convention was a well-produced show. And as it ended Clinton got a great and unexpected windfall: Ross Perot dropped out of the campaign, with little by way of a credible explanation. The combination of a successful convention and Perot's departure shot Clinton up twelve to fifteen points in the polls. He took the lead and never lost it.

By this time, President Bush, whose approval rating had been as high as 90 percent in the wake of the Persian Gulf War, was down to 37 percent, according to Gallup. The 1990–91 recession was the culprit, and though it was over by the time the general election campaign started, the recovery was slow: unemployment peaked at 7.8 percent in June 1992. The wealthy and patrician Bush, who hadn't paid a utility bill or had to go to a hardware store in the twelve years he'd lived in the vice president's home or the White House, had trouble connecting with people. Clinton, in contrast, had been telling voters "I feel your pain."

The fall campaign was in some ways anticlimactic, since Clinton stayed ahead the whole time; but twelve years is a long time to be shut out of the White House, and many Democrats couldn't quite believe that a victory was imminent. Clinton and Gore had good chemistry and campaigned well together. Bush swung at wild pitches. He called Clinton and Gore "a couple of bozos" at one point, and the way it came out it sounded overly defensive. Stan Greenberg recalled, "I think Bush couldn't believe that this guy, this draft dodger, could really beat him. They were convinced they could bring him down on trust. We were convinced the voters had factored all that in." Greenberg believes in retrospect that the Bush camp made an error in opening its campaign with attacks on Clinton's character. The Bush team should have instead attacked Clinton's record, which, since he'd led a small, poor state about which any number of unflattering statistics could be turned up, might have been more resonant.

On October 1, a potential problem arose, or re-arose: Perot got back in the race. The Clinton team was concerned that he might shake up the race in ways that couldn't be anticipated, but

Perot was more spoiler than contender at this point, with his support in polls at about 15 percent. He was, however, invited to participate in the presidential debates. The most important single moment of the general election campaign came in the second debate, on October 15, when a woman in the audience asked the candidates, "How has the national debt personally affected each of your lives?" Bush didn't seem to understand the question, which admittedly was confusing. (The woman appeared, in fact, to mean "the deficit" or perhaps simply "the weak economy.") Clinton walked to the edge of the stage, locked eyes with the woman, and delivered one of those perfect empathetic answers that politicians always strive for but rarely achieve. "I've been governor of a small state for twelve years," he said, and "in my state, when people lose their jobs, there's a good chance I'll know them by their names. When a factory closes, I know the people who ran it. When the businesses go bankrupt, I know them."

In a foreshadowing of what was to come over the next eight years, some in the media and on the right tried to call attention to various allegations against Clinton. Congressman Bob Dornan, a California Republican, took to the floor of the House of Representatives to charge that Clinton had protested against U.S. involvement in Vietnam while on his trip to the Soviet Union during his time at Oxford and had perhaps even met with KGB agents while there to conspire against America. Dornan acknowledged he had no proof, but the way the story grew provided a textbook example of how allegations with no evidence to support them could gain footing. The conservative *Washington Times* ran a "news story" on Dornan's antics, then conservative talk radio picked it up, then the Bush campaign decided to use it to attack Clinton; finally, the campaign was forced to respond. It didn't do Clinton any damage, but he should have taken note of the process by which this new kind of sausage was made.

Meanwhile, Colonel Holmes of the University of Arkansas ROTC wrote a memorandum that was read into the *Congressional Record* stating that he felt compelled to insert himself into the campaign because of "the imminent danger to our country of a draft dodger becoming Commander-in-Chief of the Armed Forces of the United States." And the *New York Times* published many stories about Whitewater; it had a funny smell to it, with the titillating nugget that Jim McDougal later became a failed savings and loan operator and that Clinton may have leaned on state bank regulators to help him out. But it was far too complicated to be converted by the Republicans into red meat.

In the end, Clinton won handily: he got 43 percent of the popular vote to Bush's 37.5 percent and Perot's 19 percent. The electoral college tally was a rout: Clinton 370, Bush 168. The six high-population states that Bush had won in 1988—California, Illinois, Pennsylvania, Michigan, New Jersey, and Maryland—were flipped by Clinton to the Democratic column, and through 2012 they would never flip back. He won four states of the former Confederacy—Georgia, Louisiana, Tennessee, and his native Arkansas—along with Kentucky and Missouri. He had sold middle Americans on the idea that they could trust the Democratic Party again. And the Republicans, who had come to believe that the White House was somehow "theirs," didn't like it a bit.

3

The New Realities of Politics

Clinton may have won the electoral college handily, but that 43 percent popular vote total was seized on by the Republicans to diminish or even delegitimize his victory. Senate majority leader Bob Dole of Kansas wasted no time conveying the message. On election night itself, Dole denied on television that Clinton had been given any kind of mandate, saying, "Put our votes together with Ross Perot, and we have a majority of the American people." (What "we" did he mean? Clinton was the second choice of about half of Perot's voters, so Dole's assumption that a Perot voter was automatically part of an anti-Clinton coalition was off base.) Dole having covered the mandate of the people, Paul Weyrich, a religious conservative who had coined the term *moral majority*, turned his attention to the mandate of heaven, announcing that an America governed by a man such as Clinton "deserves the hatred of God."

Signs of divine disapprobation were, however, few on Inauguration Day 1993. The weather was balmy enough that January day that Clinton wore no overcoat as he delivered his brief address, telling the crowd: "We have heard the trumpets. We have changed the guard." Maya Angelou read a poem—Kennedy's Robert Frost recast for a more multicultural age. The Clintons made appearances at nearly a dozen balls, including, in more generational signposting, one sponsored by MTV, where the president's brother, Roger, sang

Sam Cooke's "A Change Is Gonna Come." The next day brought another symbolic gesture as the Clintons welcomed regular Americans into the White House to say hello.

It wasn't long, though, before the clouds gathered. There were some cabinet-appointment problems, most notably with regard to the attorney general post. Clinton's first choice, Zoe Baird, withdrew her name after it was revealed that she and her husband had hired undocumented immigrants to work as their nanny and driver and had not paid their Social Security taxes. Incredibly, the "nannygate" issue also felled Clinton's second choice, Kimba Wood, a New York judge. Wood had at least paid the required taxes for her undocumented employee, but in a scandal climate, such details don't matter as much as they should.

But these were small explosions. A stick of dynamite detonated during the new president's first few days in office, when information was leaked to newspapers about the administration's plan to allow gay men and lesbians to serve openly in the military. Clinton had pledged this change in policy on the campaign trail, and the leaks had conveyed the impression that Clinton intended to steamroll the Joint Chiefs of Staff on this issue and, weirdly, that this matter had somehow bubbled up as his top priority, superseding even the economy. It was about what many Americans expected of this draft-dodging military-hater.

On January 25, 1993, Clinton had his first meeting with the Joint Chiefs, led by chairman Colin Powell, at the height of his public popularity in the aftermath of the successful Persian Gulf War. They came to the Roosevelt Room to let the new president know, as George Stephanopoulos put it, that "keeping this promise will cost you the military. Fight, and you'll lose—and it won't be pretty." A bipartisan group of senators, led by Democrats Sam Nunn of Georgia and Robert Byrd of West Virginia, came to the White House to send the message that any legislation along these lines had no chance of passage whatsoever. Clinton shelved the matter for six months to work out a compromise, but the damage had been done: this issue, which deeply divided the country and made millions feel squeamish, dominated coverage of the administration's very first days. The man who had created the Sister Souljah moment now looked as if he had, in fact, come to Washington to prostrate himself—and the United States military—before the very "special interests" from which he'd taken pains to distance himself as a candidate.

In reality, Clinton spent very little time on the issue. He pushed to deliver on some other campaign promises, notably the Family and Medical Leave Act, which provided twelve weeks of unpaid leave for any employee needing the time to attend to her own medical needs or those of a family member. The legislation had been bottled up by the threat of a veto by President Bush, and the Democratic Congress wasted no time in passing the bill once Clinton was sworn in. The new president signed it into law on February 5. But Clinton spent most of his time working on his main promise: fixing the economy and preparing his first budget. But here, too, governing proved a lot more complicated than campaigning.

The problems had started to present themselves even before Clinton took office. At a meeting of his economic team in Little Rock on January 7, 1993, advisers briefed Clinton on the latest economic indicators and informed him that various elements of his economic plan were unworkable. During the campaign, Clinton had proposed both rapid deficit reduction and a middle-class tax cut. After this meeting, he grumpily accepted the reality that it was impossible to do both. Within days, the tax cut was dropped. The Beltway arbiters of conventional wisdom, for whom deficit reduction is a perennial obsession, applauded the move, but it did constitute a reversal on a major—if irresponsible to begin with—campaign promise. The discussion at the meeting gave the president-elect a sober sense of the limitations faced even by a president, leading in time to an outburst on his part that would later become famous: "You mean to tell me that the success of my program and my reelection hinges on the Federal Reserve and a bunch of fucking bond traders?"

The underlying economic dynamic Clinton was wrestling with

was intensely political as well. This argument within the Democratic Party over whether it was more important to balance the budget or stimulate the economy through greater spending goes back at least to Franklin Roosevelt. Roosevelt was always wary of too much deficit spending (until World War II, anyway), and his famous brains trust was divided between fiscal hawks and those favoring the more Keynesian approach of robust government spending. But the debate took on special urgency in Clinton's time for two reasons.

First, he was a New Democrat who had pledged that he was going to do things in a new way—that is, not tax and spend. Second, the deficit, usually a manageable problem in postwar America, had grown larger than it had ever been since the end of World War II. In 1993 it stood at $255 billion, or around $430 billion in 2015 dollars, and had nearly quadrupled since Ronald Reagan took office in 1981. The 1993 deficit was 3.7 percent of the nation's gross domestic product, higher than the sustainable target of 3 percent set by most economists. Clinton made repeated promises during the campaign that he would cut the deficit in half in five years.

Clinton had surrounded himself with forceful personalities on both sides of the issue: Treasury secretary Lloyd Bentsen and chief economic adviser Robert Rubin as deficit hawks; secretary of labor Robert Reich and most of the political team in favor of increased spending. But as early as that January 7 meeting, Clinton had decided that the deficit hawks had the better case. "If we didn't get the deficit down substantially, interest rates would remain high, preventing a sustained, strong economic recovery," he said. By mid-February, Clinton was presenting his plan to the American people, first in a short address from the Oval Office, and then, two nights later, in an address to Congress. The plan, as all such plans are, was huge with many moving parts, touching on nearly every aspect of governance from education to law enforcement and the rest, but fiscally it boiled down to $255 billion in spending cuts and $241 billion in tax increases, mostly but not wholly on the well-off, in the name of reducing the deficit by $140 billion in five years. The package was generally well received by nonpartisan experts. The Republicans were another matter.

February ended in violence when a bomb exploded in the underground parking areas of the World Trade Center in New York City. The bombers had hoped to bring down both towers, killing thousands, but the explosion didn't prove powerful enough to do that: the damage was relatively minor, and only six people were killed. But more than a thousand were injured, and the United States had its first taste of Islamic fundamentalist terrorism on American soil.

• • •

Clinton had learned during the campaign that there were two new realities of politics that no president had quite had to deal with before. The first was a more tenacious and invasive news media. In the old days, the political reporters, nearly all men, would have agreed not to write about Gennifer Flowers and such matters. Now everything was fair game. It was the start of the era of 24/7 media culture. CNN, which had existed since 1980, had become an influential force following its wall-to-wall coverage of the 1991 Persian Gulf War; even supermarket tabloids wrote about the new first family with gusto, running articles that fed an apparent mass desire for gossip about the Clintons that played into the presumptive caricatures: Bill as a horndog cracker, Hillary as a shrewish lesbian (in spirit if not in fact), Chelsea as a maladjusted preteen chess piece moved around the board by her parents as their unquenchable thirst for power required.

There was one other new media entity: the conservative media. In 1987, the Reagan administration eliminated the Fairness Doctrine, which since the New Deal had forced broadcasters using public airwaves to give equal time to conservative and liberal viewpoints. It is interesting in retrospect to note that some conservatives feared this move, on the grounds that the liberal media would dispense with representing the conservative viewpoint entirely. But it didn't take long for broadcasters to see that conservative rage drew listeners, while liberal pieties did not. Rush Limbaugh, who had once worked as director of promotions for the Kansas City Royals and had hosted a Sacramento-based political radio show since 1984, went national in 1988. His ratings went through the roof, and many imitators soon followed. Propagandists and not journalists, Limbaugh and crew would say just about anything to bring their listeners' blood to a boil over the latest assault on America launched by blacks or professors or feminists—or Clintons.

This avowedly ideological media was just one piece of a broader right-wing infrastructure that conservative multimillionaires had begun seeding in the early 1970s, when they feared they were losing control of the country, and that had only recently begun to show results. Conservative think tanks now produced their own social science to counter that of the Brookings Institution and other venerated research organizations; conservative training and leadership institutes popped up to advance conservative reinterpretations of what had previously been settled history; organizations that were once business oriented but basically nonpartisan, such as the U.S. Chamber of Commerce, were reengineered as cogs in the conservative machine. Politics had never been a game of patty cake, but now it was becoming perpetual partisan war, at exactly the same time the mainstream media were developing an insatiable appetite for scandal.

While in Los Angeles in May 1993, Clinton decided he needed a haircut. He couldn't walk into a regular barbershop, so he decided to have his hair cut aboard Air Force One. But first he asked his Secret Service detail to make sure that the brief delay wouldn't affect air traffic at Los Angeles International Airport. He thought nothing of it and had expected to get good press out of the trip, which had involved his playing in a pickup basketball game in the African American neighborhood of South Central. Instead, he woke up the next morning to see that the newspapers had grabbed on to the fact that he'd had his hair cut by a fancy, one-named Hollywood stylist (true—Cristophe), that it had cost $200 (not true), and that he had mangled air traffic for hours (also not true).

An earlier controversy had revolved around the Clintons' decision—unusual and maybe politically unwise, but hardly scandalous—to replace the employees of the White House travel office. The Clintons said that an FBI investigation had revealed financial improprieties, but critics charged that their real motivation was to install their cronies in cushy jobs. (Three years later, the head of the travel office whom the Clintons had fired was indicted for embezzlement, but he was acquitted at trial.)

The conservative media revved itself into overdrive when Clinton nominated University of Pennsylvania law professor Lani Guinier to be associate attorney general for civil rights. Guinier was one of the country's leading theorists on voting rights, civil rights, and the problems of voter disenfranchisement—which is to say, she'd left a long paper trail for opponents to sort through. Though she explicitly opposed racial quotas as a way of redressing discrimination, she was instantly dubbed the "quota queen." Warned by his friend (and fellow Arkansan) Senator David Pryor that Guinier didn't have the votes to be confirmed, Clinton withdrew her nomination, which infuriated many African American supporters.

Matters like these pseudo-scandals, combined with the wrong-footed start on gays in the military, gave the American public a negative impression of the new administration. Clinton describes an encounter with a disillusioned voter in that bumpy first year, who demanded to know how the new president was spending his workdays.

> When he asked how much time I'd spent on gays in the military, and I told him just a few hours, he simply replied, "I don't believe you." All he knew was what he read and saw.

This was not a problem that would fade away.

• • •

Summer brought the new president's first opportunity to shape the direction of the Supreme Court, when associate justice Byron White retired. White was a moderate justice, liberal on some questions (federalism) and conservative on others (criminal procedure). His departure gave Clinton a chance to nudge the court leftward. He first offered the job to Mario Cuomo, who would surely have been a forceful liberal presence, but Cuomo turned Clinton down. The president then chose Ruth Bader Ginsburg of the United States Court of Appeals for the District of Columbia Circuit, the second-most powerful court in the country. Ginsburg quickly became a reliable liberal on the Supreme Court, but at the time of the nomination she was viewed as more of a moderate, which Clinton emphasized in introducing her in June: Ginsburg, he said, "cannot be called a liberal or a conservative; she has proved herself too thoughtful for such labels." It took just two months for the Senate to confirm her by a vote of 96 to 3.

But the main event of the summer of 1993 was the showdown over Clinton's budget. In 1981, 63 House Democrats (out of 244) had joined all House Republicans in supporting Ronald Reagan's first budget. In the Republican-controlled Senate, Reagan's budget passed overwhelmingly, with 30 Democratic votes. By 1993, though, times had changed. The Clinton budget failed to get a single Republican vote in either chamber, and indeed many Democrats from swing states (in the Senate) or districts (in the House) were afraid to support the budget because of the tax increases it included.

The Clinton plan left marginal income tax rates the same for the vast majority of filers but called for a small increase on dollars earned by individuals starting at $53,000 (about $87,000 in 2015 dollars), and then more substantial increases starting at $110,000 ($190,000, adjusted for inflation). There was a 1 percent increase in the corporate tax rate, along with some new limits on deductions. The budget included a 4.3-cent hike in the gasoline tax, the only tax that directly hit middle-class people, costing the average family around $45 a year. And its arguably most notable feature was a dramatic expansion of the Earned Income Tax Credit (EITC), a program that dated to the mid-1970s that gave a tax credit to working-poor families to lessen and in some cases eliminate their federal tax burden. Clinton's position was that anyone who worked full-time at minimum wage should exist above the poverty level, and so the EITC grew in 1993 from being a modest helping hand to "a major antipoverty initiative."

The votes, which took place in early August, were nail-biters. In the Senate, Bob Kerrey, perhaps still smarting a little from the presidential campaign, made Clinton twist in the wind for days before agreeing to vote yes. Six of the chamber's 56 Democrats defected to vote against their president, and Vice President Gore had to cast the vote that broke the 50–50 tie and got the bill through. In the House, the Republican wall of opposition and 41 Democratic defections had the White House sweating bullets, but Representative Marjorie Margolies-Mezvinsky, from a swing district in suburban Philadelphia, cast the deciding yes vote. Democrats cheered her as her "yea" registered on the big screen above the House floor. Republicans serenaded her with "Goodbye, Margie." And, sure enough, she lost the next election. In *My Life*, Clinton writes that she earned "an honored place in history." (In the silver linings department, the familial bonhomie forged that night never died—in 2010, Margolies-Mezvinsky's son, Marc, would marry Chelsea Clinton.)

It was a great victory for the president—ever since, he and Democrats have boasted that it was this budget that led to the recovery and boom of the late 1990s. And it was a great relief, because to have lost that fight would have sent the new administration into a tailspin. But all the deals the administration cut in return for yes votes came at a price, according to journalist Joe Klein: "As a result of these tactical retreats, Clinton soon gained the reputation—in Washington at least—of being a weak president, one who could be rolled." Republicans would make a mental note of this.

With the budget passed, Washington's attention turned to the North American Free Trade Agreement (NAFTA). Clinton's New Democrat credentials as a candidate were predicated on a number of departures from party orthodoxy, but without question the two biggest were his support for welfare reform and for free trade with Canada and Mexico. Welfare reform would take a while, but the administration wanted to get NAFTA done in the first year. President Bush had negotiated the agreement, but the Democrats in Congress had sat on it, bucked up by the ferocious opposition of the labor unions that helped sustain the party. But now a Democratic president was taking on most of his own party and the unions that had played a big role in his victory.

Internal White House debate centered not so much on whether the administration should pursue NAFTA; it had been a key campaign pledge, and it had to be fulfilled. Instead, it was about the efficacy and wisdom of doing it now rather than other things—specifically, instead of health care reform, which was Hillary's baby. It had been a mere five days into his presidency that Clinton announced that his wife would head his health care task force, and she had worked for months with Ira Magaziner, the president's old friend and a fellow 1968 Rhodes scholar, crafting a plan that she hoped to unveil soon. But Lloyd Bentsen at Treasury again intervened on behalf of taking the conservative path. As journalist John Harris tells it:

> At a cabinet meeting, [Bentsen] slammed his fist down on the table for emphasis in front of the president. The gesture stilled the room. NAFTA was not merely good policy, he argued, it was shaping into a critical test of the president's own principles. Did he have the nerve to fight for them?

The push was on. Clinton and Gore held hundreds of meetings with Democratic legislators, who had leverage over the White House and used it, asking for special favors for employers in their districts, many of which were granted. But there was another problem—public opinion. On November 9, 1993, the *Los Angeles Times* reported the results of a Gallup poll showing 38 percent in support of the treaty and 46 percent opposed.

That very November 9, a Tuesday, turned out to be an important date. It was that night that Gore, defending the treaty, faced off on

CNN's *Larry King Live* against Ross Perot, the former presidential candidate who was also NAFTA's most prominent critic. Intense hype had preceded the debate, and the general expectation was that Perot, who'd certainly held his own with Clinton and Bush in the previous fall's debates, was going to wipe the floor with Gore. Instead the opposite happened. The debate was scrappy, contentious, and at times rude. But the verdict was clear: Gore was more composed, Perot more flustered, and Gore had made the better case. On November 18, the House passed NAFTA, 234 to 200. More Democrats voted against than for, 156 to 102, but the Republican margin in favor was substantial (132 to 43). The Senate passed the bill easily three days later. Clinton had kept a major campaign promise but opened up an intraparty debate that continues to raise blood pressures on both sides of the argument.

• • •

On a range of fronts, Clinton kept pushing. Just after Thanksgiving 1993, Congress passed the Brady bill, which mandated background checks and waiting periods for firearms purchases. It was named for James Brady, President Reagan's press secretary, who had been grievously wounded in the 1981 assassination attempt that nearly killed Reagan, but for years the legislation had been held up in Congress by the Republicans.

Earlier in the fall, Clinton had signed the law creating his AmeriCorps program to enable young people to spend a year performing community service. And in the greatest foreign policy coup of his early presidency, he hosted Israeli prime minister Yitzhak Rabin and Palestinian leader Yasser Arafat at the White House after Israeli and Palestinian negotiators had completed the Oslo framework for a peace settlement. Clinton was justifiably proud of that moment—and justifiably worried about the stagecraft. He got Rabin, however reluctantly, to agree to shake Arafat's hand in front of the Rose Garden cameras, but both Clinton and Rabin were mortified at the thought that Arafat would attempt a double-cheek kiss, the traditional Arab greeting. Clinton spent time with his aides portraying the two principals, practicing how he would grab Arafat gently by the arm to prevent him from leaning in for the buss.

But the artillery shells kept coming. The *Washington Post* and the *New York Times* kept publishing stories about the Whitewater deal—stories that proved nothing but suggested plenty. Over the course of the fall, cries began to mount for Attorney General Janet Reno to appoint a special prosecutor to look into whether the Clintons (as investors) had done anything illegal, or whether Bill Clinton (as governor) had pressured state officials to do favors for the couple's coinvestors, Jim McDougal and his wife, Susan.

As the administration marched toward completing its first year, the internal debate on whether to accede to this demand moved to center stage. Bernard Nussbaum, the White House counsel, argued strenuously against a special prosecutor, saying—presciently, it turned out—that a prosecutor with an unlimited budget would keep turning over rocks until he found *something*. David Gergen, the erstwhile Republican presidential aide whom Clinton had asked in mid-1993 to come in and bring some order to the playgroundish chaos that had reigned in the early months, agreed with Nussbaum but advised Clinton to turn over all the pertinent records to the media. George Stephanopoulos and deputy chief of staff Harold Ickes, sensing inevitability, suggested that Clinton just go ahead and get it over with. Clinton himself didn't want to, mostly on constitutional and statutory grounds; the independent counsel law stipulated that one should be named only when there existed "credible evidence" of wrongdoing, which did not exist. "My instincts," he wrote, "were to release the records and fight the prosecutor, but if the consensus was to do the reverse, I could live with it."

And so, on January 7, 1994, word got out that Reno favored the appointment of a special prosecutor: to investigate Whitewater and, preposterously, the suicide of Vince Foster, a White House aide who had killed himself in July 1993 after having been the subject of a series of innuendo-rich editorials in the *Wall Street*

Journal, which speculated that he'd skirted the law on a number of fronts, and even groused about Foster's failure to supply the *Journal* with a photograph of himself in a timely way. Foster was a former law partner of Hillary's at the Rose Law Firm in Little Rock, and as a child he had been little Billy Blythe's neighbor and oldest friend.

So Clinton chose to live with it—and, four years later, nearly died by it.

4

———

The Limits of Power

Foreign policy hadn't been much of an issue in the 1992 campaign. The Cold War was over and won. The Berlin Wall had come down in 1989, and the Soviet Union itself, the great ideological foe of seven decades whose mere presence had done so much to define U.S. foreign policy, domestic policy, and even societal culture, had ceased to be on Christmas Day 1991. Islamic fundamentalism existed, certainly, but it was mostly a regional problem. Anxiety about the state of the world was low, while anxiety about the state of the economy was high.

The Cold War victory was sweet, but it had created a paradoxical problem for the American military, and for the American foreign policy establishment more generally: What were they to do now? The Soviet Union's existence had made their raison d'être clear; now what? What was a hegemonic military in a comparatively stable world supposed to do with itself, and what should the new imperatives of American foreign policy be? These were the urgent questions of the day. Many spoke of "humanitarian intervention" as a new course for America, inserting the military into desperate situations around the world to save lives, and to do so in places where U.S. strategic interests were not directly threatened—a clear break from Cold War realpolitik. A darker current, housed in President Bush's Defense Department, which was led by Dick Cheney,

argued that the United States would still face unforeseeable smaller
threats and that it might have to start a preemptive war or two to
show the world who was boss.

Clinton, like any governor, lacked foreign policy experience. But
in his case the situation was worse. The draft issue made it difficult for a significant percentage of Americans to imagine him as a
credible commander in chief. And his reputation as a shifty pol
who would say whatever was needed to please audiences didn't
help. On the campaign trail Clinton tried to argue that he'd supported the Persian Gulf War, the only war the United States had
won since World War II. But the *Chicago Tribune* was not alone in
observing that "his campaign has not been able to produce any evidence that puts Clinton squarely on record behind the president's
policy before the war started." A quote from early 1991 failed to
clarify matters. "I guess I would have voted with the majority if it
was a close vote," Clinton said of the congressional vote to autho-
rize that war. "But I agree with the arguments the minority made."
Nevertheless, the voters placed the world in his hands.

The most pressing global crisis was Bosnia. Yugoslavia had
been cobbled together by the great powers after World War I. It
was the convergence point of three distinct religion-based cultures:
Roman Catholicism, Eastern Orthodoxy, and the remnants of
Islam from the days of the Ottoman Empire. During most of the
Cold War, Yugoslavia was neither East nor West, and only a dictator
such as Josip Broz Tito was able to hold its patchwork of ethnici-
ties and religions together. When the Cold War ended, the place
exploded. The different regions declared their independence as
nations. The new republic of about four million people called Bosnia and Herzegovina was plurality Muslim but multiethnic, with a
large Serbian population within its borders. Bosnia's leaders sought
to build a pluralistic society, but next door in the larger and stronger Serbia, the new leader, Slobodan Milosevic, a remorselessly
chauvinistic nationalist, saw matters differently, especially with
regard to the Bosnian Serbs.

In the spring of 1992, after a series of diplomatic failures, fight-

ing broke out. The Serbs laid siege to Sarajevo, the Bosnian capital
and one of the most gloriously beautiful cities of southern Europe.
A new phrase entered the political lexicon: *ethnic cleansing*, the dis-
placement, torture, and slaughter of thousands of civilians on
account of their ethnic identity. It was the worst violence on European soil since World War II, and while the Serbs weren't the only
ones with blood on their hands, Milosevic drew comparisons, not
wholly inapt, to Hitler. Western intellectuals such as Susan Son-
tag and Christopher Hitchens demanded a humanitarian intervention. But the Bush administration, whose policy of refraining from
direct involvement in post–Cold War European matters had for the
most part served it well, did nothing. As Bush's secretary of state
James Baker had said to Congress: "We don't have a dog in this
fight."

Baker was an old-school, Cold War–era realist. Clinton's worldview was more informed by his generational experiences—
including Vietnam and the rise of human rights as a legitimate
concern—and his view of the Balkans conflict reflected that. During the presidential campaign, he'd come out in favor of NATO air
strikes against Serbian aggression and of lifting a 1991 arms embargo
that had been imposed on all parties but affected the new Bosnian
state most adversely.

As this was mostly a European matter, the views of America's
European allies mattered, too. Germany's Helmut Kohl was mostly
with Clinton, but Britain's John Major and France's François
Mitterrand were implacably opposed to anything that might esca-
late the violence. So NATO couldn't agree on a course of action, and
neither for the most part could the United Nations, since Russia,
Serbia's chief ally, could be assured of vetoing any strongly anti-
Serbian action on the Security Council. The UN, however, had
established a no-fly zone, and when four Serbian aircraft violated
it in February 1994, NATO jets shot them down. In May of that
year, the Senate passed, at Bob Dole's behest, a resolution urging
that the United States unilaterally lift the arms embargo. Clinton
was reluctant to do this, he writes in *My Life*, because he thought

unilateral action would weaken the UN and because he "didn't want to divide the NATO alliance." Clinton brought in the veteran diplomat Richard Holbrooke to try to sort the mess out, but the conflict ground on. The real showdown with Milosevic would come a few years—and many thousands of dead bodies—later.

As bad as things were in the Balkans, the single biggest foreign policy catastrophe of the early Clinton years happened elsewhere— in Somalia. A civil war had ravaged the country for two years, devastating the population and rendering Somalia (in another new phrase from the era) a "failed state." Calls for humanitarian intervention arose, and in December 1992, during his final weeks in office, President Bush responded. He ordered a deployment of 28,000 American troops into Somalia, promising that they "will not stay one day longer than is absolutely necessary."

Inevitably, it dragged on. In October 1993, U.S. Delta Forces launched an assault on the militia of strongman Mohamed Farah Aidid in Mogadishu, the capital. Aidid's men shot down two UH-60 Black Hawk helicopters, killing eighteen American soldiers—at the time, the largest single-day loss of life for the United States since Vietnam. American news broadcasts showed images of Somalis dragging American soldiers' bodies through the barren capital's streets. Clinton told his aides he couldn't believe "we're being pushed around by these two-bit pricks." He got the United States disentangled fast, as public opinion demanded. Americans decided that they'd better think twice about these humanitarian interventions, but Americans weren't the only ones watching; a little-known Islamic fundamentalist based in Sudan named Osama bin Laden made a mental note that the great United States seemed to have no stomach for death.

The Mogadishu tragedy would have further disastrous consequences a few months later, when the Clinton administration made no effort to stop a genocide in the tiny East African nation of Rwanda in the spring of 1994. For three months the majority Hutu government of Rwanda slaughtered as much as 70 percent of the minority Tutsi population, along with many moderate Hutus.

While it's impossible to know how much of the bloodshed the United States could have prevented, we do know that Clinton never once convened his top foreign policy advisers to discuss the issue.

The final foreign policy crisis of Clinton's early tenure unfolded in Haiti, where a duly elected president, Jean-Bertrand Aristide, had been deposed in a coup d'état in 1991. Aristide had been popularly elected in the wake of the collapse of the brutal François Duvalier dictatorship; he was a man of the left who had vowed to challenge the established order in the Western Hemisphere's poorest nation. After a mere eight months, the military overthrew him. The new regime of Raoul Cédras crushed the aspirations of the people and cut a lurid swath of rape and murder and torture (lacerating mothers' faces as their children watched) across Haiti. Clinton attempted diplomacy while also imposing sanctions. In July 1993, Cédras signed an agreement saying he would give up power. He did not, and by September 1994, Clinton had made his decision—he would use American military force to put Aristide back in the presidential palace. During the Cold War, the United States had propped up the sanguinary Duvaliers because they were anticommunist. Now Clinton was ordering the United States military to bring a leftist back to power. It sure wasn't the Cold War anymore.

It was a brave and risky (and, to critics, foolhardy) decision on Clinton's part: American public opinion was firmly against using the military in this way. The Pentagon opposed the intervention as well. But the mission was accomplished with no loss of life, setting a precedent that the United States was capable of a quick and successful humanitarian intervention, provided success was measured as accomplishing a limited mission and not transforming the society. Haiti did not become a paradise, but Aristide went on to serve his country as president twice, and the nation has seen some improvements on political pluralism, civil liberties, and the rule of law.

In confronting these three foreign policy crises early in his term, Clinton helped define the priorities of a post–Cold War America. Beyond these, a range of calamities asserted themselves. In June

1994, North Korea began removing weapons-grade plutonium, five or six bombs' worth, from fuel rods at a research reactor. The world came closer than it knew in June 1994 to full-scale war on the Korean peninsula—the Clinton administration very seriously considered a preemptive strike against the North's nuclear reactor at Yongbyon, and it feared that such an action would provoke Pyongyang to attack the South. It was former president Jimmy Carter's fortuitous presence in the North Korean capital, where he was meeting with dictator Kim Il Sung as a private citizen, that helped stave off hostilities. Carter hustled to find a diplomatic answer.

Events in Northern Ireland also took the new president, and the world, somewhat by surprise. In November 1993, word was leaked that the British government and the Irish Republican Army (IRA), which had been in a virtual state of war since 1969, had been engaged in secret cease-fire talks. The revelation damaged British prime minister John Major, but the next month Major and Albert Reynolds, his Irish counterpart whose government had also been in secret talks with the Provisional IRA, signed the Downing Street Declaration, which provided a framework for an IRA cease-fire and, down the road, potential Irish unification. This placed in Clinton's lap the delicate issue of whether to grant Sinn Féin leader Gerry Adams a visa to visit the United States—something utterly unheard of for a Northern Irish leader (or terrorist, depending on how one saw things). Adams's very voice had been banned from the BBC since 1988. Britain, by far America's closest ally, lobbied furiously against the visa. But Clinton became convinced that Adams was serious about peace, and he granted the visa. It was a gamble that enraged conservatives and infuriated John Major, who didn't take Clinton's phone calls for weeks, but it was one that history would largely reward.

. . .

For Bill Clinton, as for most presidents, foreign policy decisions were often made in response to unpredictable world events; in the realm over which the president had more opportunity to take the initiative, domestic policy, there was a clear top priority for 1994: health care reform.

The priority had been established by Clinton's presidential campaign, and by history. Health care reform, specifically the idea of some kind of universal health insurance coverage, was the one piece of great unfinished business from the New Deal era. The nations of Europe had all initiated different forms of universal coverage, but in the United States what developed was a system in which health coverage was tied to one's job. Lyndon Johnson got Congress to pass socialized medicine for the elderly (Medicare) in 1965, but the insurance lobbies, which under any government-administered system would stand to lose millions of customers, were powerful enough to block anything more comprehensive.

Health care reform mostly disappeared as an issue in American politics during the 1970s and '80s. But over the course of the 1980s, things started to change: costs increased; insurers and employers began to shift more of the burden of those costs to customers; and more people lost their insurance altogether. Still, public frustration was diffuse, and no one campaigned on it, until a special election in Pennsylvania for the U.S. Senate in 1991, when the Democrat, Harris Wofford, rode the issue to an upset victory over the heavily favored Republican, Dick Thornburgh. Two of Wofford's advisers, James Carville and Paul Begala, would go on to hold senior positions in Clinton's 1992 campaign, and they saw in health care a winning issue for Clinton.

So Clinton campaigned hard on reform and put Hillary in charge of the effort at the beginning of his presidency. The budget and NAFTA may have taken precedence in 1993, but the First Lady and Ira Magaziner assembled a task force in the administration's early days that conducted public hearings around the country and private meetings in Washington. The latter provided a fat target, as the administration's foes, led by the editorial page of the *Wall Street Journal*, promoted lurid gossip about what manner of socialistic evils the First Lady was up to behind closed doors. The nascent conservative movement was against any efforts at reform, but

Republicans in Congress weren't, necessarily; according to Clinton, Senate Republican leader Bob Dole was telling him privately that a compromise could be worked out.

In September 1993, Clinton tried to kick-start the effort with a speech to a joint session of Congress that had not, at first, gone auspiciously. When the president stood at the rostrum to begin his speech, he noticed that the teleprompter in front of him was scrolling the wrong text; it had been loaded with a previous speech he'd given to Congress months before. It was seven or so minutes before his aides loaded the right text into the device, minutes during which Clinton delivered the speech extemporaneously—and expertly. Maybe his improvisational skills could get a bill passed, too.

The principles of reform he laid out in that speech were centered on the idea of "managed competition." The marketplace for health coverage would still be a private one, but the government would manage the competition to structure and adjust the market, to establish equitable rules, and more. The end goals were universal coverage and cost control. The president tried to sum it all up in six words: "security, simplicity, savings, choice, quality, and responsibility."

The speech polled favorably but, out of public view, all was not well. Hillary and Magaziner drew heavy criticism, some of it legitimate and some from people with axes of their own to grind, for being haughty or dismissive of both policy and political advice. Daniel Patrick Moynihan, the esteemed New York senator through whose committee any legislation would have to proceed, felt that he had not been treated with the deference he deserved, and he let the administration know of his unhappiness by making negative comments about the process on NBC's *Meet the Press*.

And Hillary's role, controversial from the start, came under increasing fire—not just from Republicans, but from fellow Democrats who thought she was politically maladroit and too unwilling to compromise. Some within the administration believed the emotional and psychological dynamic at play between the president and the First Lady had a big influence on the final shape of the policy. Continuing gossip about Bill's infidelities and his guilt that Hillary was being dragged through the mud on matters such as Whitewater made the president more likely to put aside his own political judgment (which was sharper than his wife's) and accede to all of her desires. This dynamic, David Gergen told John Harris, put Clinton "in a situation where on health care he never challenged it in a way he ordinarily would have, had he been under a different psychological situation."

At the same time that outsiders were criticizing the process, the divisions within the administration over policy substance were stark, and the internal debates ferocious. Again it was the economic team, led by Lloyd Bentsen, that expressed the deepest reservations about the plan. Placing caps on premiums, the economic advisers pointed out, reeked of "price controls," which Congress hated. After losing a series of internal arguments in the fall of 1993, Bentsen personally handed Hillary Clinton a memo expressing his misgivings about the health care plan; it was thirty-eight single-spaced pages long. Hillary, wrote journalist Elizabeth Drew, "scathingly dismissed behind their backs those who wanted to go slower—mainly, the economic advisers—as 'the incrementalists.'"

All these people were the administration's *friends*. Among its foes, the armaments were being delivered to the front. Two weeks before Clinton's speech, a lobbying group called the Health Insurance Association of America began running television ads featuring a wholesome-looking white couple, Harry and Louise, sitting at their kitchen table fretting about the changes coming with reform—that they wouldn't be able to choose their own doctors and that their premiums would rise. This was largely unfair, but Harry and Louise seemed attractive and credible. The group spent nearly $20 million running the ads for a full year.

In late 1993, the administration finally released its health care plan, which ran to 1,342 pages. It was an instant, and easy, target of attack. The number of experts who could read a document of such sprawling complexity and interpret it for Americans in good faith could literally be counted on one hand, or at most two; they were somewhat outnumbered. A scathing and award-winning (and later discredited) attack in the *New Republic* was highly influential inside the Beltway; elsewhere in the country, criticisms took hold that the plan constituted a government takeover of the health care system and was really just a new form of welfare extending a benefit to people who didn't work. Most of the criticisms were exaggerations or outright lies. At the same time, the changes proposed were indeed vast. It was reasonable for ordinary people to wonder and worry about how the changes might affect them. Public anxiety like that is very easily stoked.

Any continuing Republican openness to reform was quashed in December 1993, when Bill Kristol, a former aide to Vice President Dan Quayle and the son of the neoconservative intellectual Irving Kristol, wrote a memo to congressional Republicans urging them to move heaven and earth to block reform. Kristol warned that reform would present "a serious political threat to the Republican Party," while "unqualified political defeat of the Clinton health care proposal . . . would be a monumental setback for the president, and an incontestable piece of evidence that Democratic welfare-state liberalism remains firmly in retreat." The memo was addressed to Republicans in general, but Bob Dole was its main target. Dole was contemplating a run for president in 1996, and Kristol's memo surely clarified for him that helping Bill Clinton pass historic legislation was not going to be the best way to win Republican hearts and minds.

· · ·

The other defining legislative battle of 1994 was the crime bill. The early 1990s were a time of historically high violent crime rates— in 1990 New York City surpassed 2,000 homicides per year for the first time. Nationally, the early '90s saw 23,000 or so murders being committed every year, numbers that represented steady increases from the previous decade. Clinton, in New Democrat mode, had vowed while campaigning that he would be tougher on crime than the typical liberal and repeatedly promised that he would hire

100,000 new police officers, a measure that was the bill's center-piece.

At first, things went smoothly on this front. Clinton introduced the bill in September 1993; it sailed through the relevant committees and even passed the House by voice vote and the Senate 95 to 4. But as the two bodies met to work out the differences in their two bills, House Democrats decided to add to the broad crime bill a measure they had passed earlier by itself: an assault weapons ban on nineteen specific kinds of firearms and on new magazines that could hold more than ten rounds of ammunition. This changed matters swiftly. The National Rifle Association shifted into high gear against what it saw as an assault on the Second Amendment.

Alongside the NRA, there were Republicans in Congress who didn't want Clinton to win a major victory of any kind in advance of the 1994 midterm elections. They called attention to the bill's more liberal-sounding provisions in an effort to persuade Americans that, rhetoric aside, Clinton was just another soft-on-crime liberal. The "liberal" crime prevention provisions included items such as new money for domestic violence programs and for youth programs, which the bill's opponents characterized as "money for midnight basketball."

The NRA kept up the pressure throughout the summer of 1994. Clinton countered, cleverly, by getting police unions on his side, so that as the NRA tried to paint him as anti-gun, at least he would never be seen as anti-cop. A small number of liberal Democrats, including twelve of the thirty-nine members of the Congressional Black Caucus, opposed their president on the grounds that the law's harsher elements expanding the death penalty and limiting parole would put far more young men in prison. And many nervous Democrats came to the White House to meet with Clinton to tell him they'd like to be with him, but if they voted against the NRA, they'd be finished in any bid for reelection.

So this was Clinton's second summer as president—trying to pass these two huge signature pieces of legislation. He also was given a second opportunity to appoint a justice to the Supreme

Court, when associate justice Harry Blackmun retired. Blackmun was a solid liberal, so there was less of a chance to change the balance of the court than there had been when Byron White retired. Clinton chose Stephen Breyer, a former Harvard Law professor and a longtime judge on the federal appeals court in Boston. Like Ginsburg, Breyer was clearly qualified and had avoided writing or saying anything over the years that could serve as fodder for the right-wing judicial groups opposing him. Nine Republican senators voted against him in the end, but most agreed with Senator Phil Gramm of Texas that Breyer was "as good as we have a right to expect."

Clinton was still dealing with Whitewater, and in June—feeling that under the circumstances he could hardly veto it—he fatefully signed a bill renewing the statute that allowed independent counsels to investigate allegations of executive branch scandal. He also went to Normandy that month to commemorate the fiftieth anniversary of D-Day. On the day he returned, Senator Ted Kennedy's committee reported out a health care bill, with all Democrats and one Republican supporting it. But two days later, Bob Dole made a fateful announcement: he would see to it that Senate Republicans would block any health care legislation. Dole controlled only a minority of senators, but under the Senate's supermajority rules, any group of forty-one senators can block a piece of legislation from coming to the floor.

Leading congressional Democrats urged Clinton to take the assault-weapons provision out of the crime bill, arguing that voting for it would endanger many Democrats in the November election. Clinton stood firm. On August 21, 1994, the crime bill passed the House 235 to 195, with 64 Democrats voting against. Four days later it passed the Senate, and Clinton signed it into law on September 13—a major campaign promise fulfilled.

Health care, however, spun out in the other direction. On September 26, Senate Democratic leader George Mitchell officially threw in the towel, announcing that he would not have the votes to break Dole's promised filibuster. "Under the rules of the Senate," he said, "a minority can obstruct the majority. This is what happened to comprehensive health-insurance reform." The hand-writing had been on the wall for some time, but it was still a dev-astating day for the White House. "Maybe," Bill Clinton reflected, "I was pushing the Congress, the country, and the administration too hard."

The next day wasn't very good for Clinton, either. That was when dozens of Republican members of Congress stood on the steps of the Capitol, pledging a "Contract with America" that they would pursue legislatively if voters made them the new House majority—and made their audacious insurgent leader the new Speaker of the House.

5

The President Is Relevant

It was in May 1984, as Joe Klein tells the story in *The Natural*, his political biography of Bill Clinton, that the Newt Gingrich era in the House of Representatives began. Gingrich was a young Republican congressman from the wealthy suburbs outside Atlanta. General William Tecumseh Sherman had marched through those parts during the Civil War; ample defense contracts modernized the area during World War II. In the early 1960s, the city of Atlanta wanted to expand into Cobb County, immediately northwest of the city. County officials responded by incorporating a new "city," in many places only ten feet wide, the better to keep Atlanta—specifically, its black residents—out.

This is the milieu from which Newt Gingrich emerged. Born in Pennsylvania in 1943, Gingrich moved to Georgia as a teenager in 1960 and returned to the state in the early 1970s as a history professor with a PhD from Tulane University. The northern and western Atlanta suburbs, where he eventually planted himself, were still Democratic then, but by the 1970s they were starting to think more Republican. In 1974, Gingrich came within a whisker of unseating an entrenched Democratic congressman; he lost again, also narrowly, in 1976. But by 1978, the Democrat got the message and retired, and Gingrich became a member of Congress. He broke the mold for junior House members. So many of them struggle to

put three nonrehearsed sentences together and barely know much
of anything beyond politics, but Gingrich knew a little something
about all kinds of things. He had opinions—an explosion of them—
and he wasn't shy about delivering them at length; he also had a
taste for partisan combat and a keen instinct for the kinds of attacks
that would get juices flowing on both sides. People called him a
bomb thrower, and he didn't mind.

In May 1984, Gingrich took to the House floor and gave a speech
questioning the patriotism of several Democratic colleagues by
name. Few other members were in the chamber at the time—but
the C-SPAN cameras were there. Speaker Tip O'Neill, who came
from a time when House members simply did not call out colleagues
by name, especially for the purpose of smearing them, was apoplec-
tic when he heard about Gingrich's speech a week later. Speakers
almost never go down into the House well to orate, but O'Neill
did now, launching into a tirade against Gingrich and ordering that
thenceforth C-SPAN cameras would pan the empty chamber so
that viewers would see that speeches such as Gingrich's were
charades. A furious partisan battle ensued. The Gingrich era was
under way.

In the succeeding years, Gingrich had a hand in bringing down
O'Neill's successor as Speaker, Jim Wright, and an aide to Gingrich spread rumors about the sexual orientation of the Speaker who
followed Wright, Tom Foley. He got himself voted majority whip
by the columns of young conservative Republicans then emerging
from southern and midwestern suburbs and exurbs. He made quite
a counterpoint to the longtime Republican House leader Robert
Michel, a war hero and true old-school moderate from Peoria, Illinois, who had first come to Congress in 1957. By the time Bill
Clinton became president, Michel saw which way the partisan
winds were blowing. He complained that the younger Republicans
seemed too keen on picking fights and announced that he wouldn't
seek reelection in 1994, which teed everything up for Gingrich to
lead the party in the House and seek the speakership for himself.

The Contract with America was an audacious gamble—an

attempt to "nationalize" a midterm election, to make it about national issues rather than local ones, as had been customary. The contract was a ten-item list of measures cooked up by Gingrich and conservative pollster Frank Luntz after extensive focus grouping of Americans to see what was making them angry. It committed a Republican House majority to pass a tough-on-crime law, a law cutting welfare payments, and another to limit punitive damages in tort proceedings, along with procedural reforms that would help advance conservative causes (and please some major donors). The contract galvanized conservatives across the country, and the new conservative media, now sermonizing to a radio audience in the millions, hyped it every day. Gingrich, feeling his oats in a big way, lobbed grenade after grenade over the course of the fall, even going so far, a few days before the election, as to tie a South Carolina mother's drowning of her two young sons to a moral turpitude that was an inescapable by-product of Democratic governance and values.

Liberals, meanwhile, were dispirited. Clinton's approval rating was down to 44 percent. He knew things were looking grim, and in his extreme anxiety he privately got back in touch with Dick Morris, the strategist who had helped him regain the Arkansas governorship in 1982 but was now working with Republican candidates. Morris told Clinton that he expected the Democrats to lose the Senate, a prediction with which the president agreed. But Clinton was taken aback to hear what Morris said next.

"You're going to lose the Senate *and* the House," he said.

"Not the House," Clinton replied. "No way." The Democrats held an eighty-seat margin in the House, and Clinton was not alone in thinking this majority was impregnable.

The blowout was enormous. With a voter turnout of only about 40 percent—20 points down from the 1992 presidential election—the Republicans picked up eight Senate seats to take the majority. In the House, they gained fifty-four, well above most predictions, going from 176 seats to 230—just as Morris had predicted. The election ushered in the party's first majority in that chamber in forty years. Speaker of the House Tom Foley lost his seat, too—the first sitting Speaker to lose reelection since Reconstruction. Senator Harris Wofford of Pennsylvania, whose upset victory in 1991 on the strength of health care reform had once seemed to augur sunny days to come, lost to an ultraconservative congressman, Rick Santorum. Across the country, not a single Republican incumbent congressman, senator, or governor lost. Even the 1974 post-Watergate election hadn't seen so stark a turnover of seats. The point was not lost on Clinton that it was the worst beating the Democrats had taken since 1946—right after, he later noted in *My Life*, President Harry Truman had tried to pass universal health care.

But it wasn't just health care. The NRA claimed to have taken out around twenty Democrats because of their votes on the assault-weapons ban. And while the economy was beginning to show signs of life, they weren't yet recognizable enough for most people to notice. To Clinton himself, there were echoes of his 1980 gubernatorial defeat: he hadn't listened. He later reflected that if he'd dropped health care when he knew it was going to die anyway and pushed welfare reform, he might have salvaged things. But he didn't. Gingrich outfoxed him every step of the way.

In the face of such a thoroughgoing rejection and with no chance of passing any kind of progressive legislative agenda, the president now had to figure out how to go on being the president.

• • •

Clinton, Dole, and Gingrich made pro forma noises about working together, but Gingrich had achieved his lofty station in part by repeatedly flashing the rhetorical knife, and he wasn't about to sheathe it now. Just before the election, he'd called the president an "enemy of normal Americans"; immediately afterward he dubbed Bill and Hillary "counterculture McGoverniks." Then he charged, with no evidence, that up to 25 percent of the White House staff were recent drug users. The coming battles would be over the budget and the items in the Contract with America, but for Gingrich they were really battles for the very soul of the nation.

The Clinton White House was at sea. Hillary, known in those

days for a New Age–ish penchant for searches for "meaning" and
the like, invited to the White House and to Camp David visitors
such as pop self-help guru Tony Robbins, a wildly successful author
known for thirty-minute infomercials in which his followers walked
across hot coals. There's no evidence the president did that literally,
but he was doing enough of it metaphorically. After the election,
much of Washington didn't take him seriously anymore. Then, in
January, his economic advisers came to him with news that was
inescapably horrible from any angle: Mexico was about to default
on $30 billion worth of loans. If that happened, it would surely
mean a financial crisis of the first order, with inflation, higher
unemployment, and more. In all likelihood it would also mean a
huge wave of illegal immigration as people fled a sinking Mexico.
To prevent all that, the United States would have to extend costly
loans on easy terms. Public opinion was strongly against such a bail-
out, but substantively Clinton had no choice but to bite the bullet
and do it.

There was still more bleak January 1995 news, this time on the
Whitewater front. After Clinton had agreed to the appointment of
a special prosecutor, Attorney General Janet Reno in January 1994
named Robert B. Fiske Jr., a moderate Republican and a former federal prosecutor, to conduct the investigation. Fiske began by focus-
ing on Vince Foster's suicide. Within six months, Fiske had issued
his report: Foster was depressed and killed himself, and he wasn't
hiding anything about Whitewater or anything else related to the
Clintons' finances. Two congressional committees reached the
same conclusion.

But then came the baroque chain of events that in time would
almost drive Clinton from office. On the same day that Fiske
released his report in June 1994, Clinton signed his name to a new
independent counsel law. He hated doing it, for his own sake and
on principle; a prosecutor with unlimited time and funds amounted
to a virtual fourth branch of government unto himself. This was
an opinion held by many on both sides of the political aisle. In fact,
the case against independent counsels had been made forcefully by

conservative Supreme Court justice Antonin Scalia in 1988, when he was the lone justice to hold that such prosecutors were unconstitutional.

> An independent counsel is selected, and the scope of his or her authority prescribed, by a panel of judges. What if they are politically partisan, as judges have been known to be, and select a prosecutor antagonistic to the administration? . . . There is no remedy for that, not even a political one.

Clinton's signature on the new law had one major and fateful implication: it shifted the oversight responsibility of an independent counsel from the attorney general's office to a special three-judge panel of the U.S. Court of Appeals for the D.C. Circuit known as the Special Division. The head of this unit was David Sentelle, a conservative Republican judge who had called liberals "leftist heretics" in a journal article and whose partisan views were well known. The panel included another conservative judge, which gave them a majority. Reno forwarded Fiske's name to the Special Division, which she thought was just a pro forma move, but on August 5, 1994, the Special Division fired Fiske, citing a preposterous alleged conflict. (Fiske's huge law firm—not Fiske himself, merely the firm—had once represented International Paper, which years before had sold some product to Jim McDougal.)

The panel replaced him with Kenneth Starr, the former solicitor general under President George H. W. Bush. Starr had a good reputation in Washington social circles but also a long record of conservative activism that wasn't widely known at the time. He was also sitting on more than one potential legal conflict of interest that he did not reveal. His own huge law firm, Kirkland & Ellis, represented International Paper *at the time* of his appointment (although the firm did drop that representation after Starr was named). Fiske had given every indication that he was going to wrap up his investigation in a few months. Starr took no significant action during the election season, but in January, with Republicans in control of Congress, he announced that he was reopening the Foster investigation.

Starr's appointment was a crucial victory for a "movement" of people who were willing to say anything about Clinton—backed by rich people who were willing to pay the conspiracy mongers very well to do it. The Pittsburgh billionaire Richard Mellon Scaife funded something called the "Arkansas Project," designed to send journalists and investigators to the Natural State to dig up anything they could on Clinton, or to make things up when the digging proved fruitless. The Reverend Jerry Falwell, the founder of the Moral Majority, made a "documentary" called *The Clinton Chronicles*, which alleged that the president had had a number of people killed; the "Clinton body count" became a thing that these people actually discussed seriously. The mainstream media did not exactly embrace this nonsense, but the mere reporting on it gave the theories oxygen.

There was a darker side to all this right-wing rage, aimed not just at the Clintons but at government and even American society generally. Far-right fringe movements that trafficked in race hatred and conspiracy theories about Jews had existed for decades; a movement with an actual name, the Patriot Movement, went back to the 1950s or '60s. But two events had driven larger numbers into what was by this time called the militia movement: the 1992 raid by federal agents on the home of a survivalist named Randy Weaver, which resulted in the death of his unarmed wife and son in Ruby Ridge, Idaho; and the government's storming the following year of the compound of the Branch Davidians, a sect run by a messianic extremist named David Koresh, who had brainwashed adults, seduced underage girls, and fathered numerous children. A long standoff at the compound in Waco, Texas, finally led to a raid that resulted in seventy-six dead, more than twenty of them children. This had happened under the new Democratic president, a man who had been presumed in far-right circles to hanker to slam down the federal jackboot on the nation's throat even before such a raid.

The ranks of survivalists swelled. They especially despised the Bureau of Alcohol, Tobacco, and Firearms (ATF), which was said to be coming for everyone's guns. Books like *The Turner Diaries*, a novel by a white supremacist in which the government is over-thrown and all "undesirable" races eliminated, sold briskly. Some of the new conservative radio hosts fueled this paranoia directly: G. Gordon Liddy, the convicted Watergate conspirator, once advised his listeners that if they saw an ATF man approaching, "Go for a head shot; they're going to be wearing bulletproof vests." Republi-can officeholders fed this beast, too. Numerous southern and west-ern Republicans pandered to their constituents' fear of the federal government and showily browbeat representatives of these agen-cies who came to testify on Capitol Hill.

Clinton limped through the spring; on the night of April 18, 1995, he gave a news conference that two of the three major tele-vision networks didn't even carry live. A journalist asked him about this, and about how the Gingrich Republicans had all the energy on their side, and the president was reduced to reminding America that "the president is relevant; the Constitution gives me relevance." The next day was the two-year anniversary of the Waco raid. The White House news on the front page of that day's *New York Times* concerned the president's rejection of a Republican welfare reform bill. And then, at 9:02 a.m. central time, a bomb exploded at the Alfred P. Murrah Federal Office Building in Oklahoma City, rip-ping an exterior wall off the nine-story building. The blast killed 168 people, including 19 children who attended day care in the building.

It didn't take authorities long to identify the perpetrator, a young man named Timothy McVeigh. Barely an hour after the explosion McVeigh was stopped for a traffic violation and arrested for illegal handgun possession, so, conveniently enough, he was in jail already when the clues led authorities his way. McVeigh, a native of upstate New York, was a decorated Gulf War veteran whose antigovern-ment instincts had grown more intense after he left the service; the Waco raid had radicalized him completely, and he'd vowed to exact revenge.

Before the bombing he had written a letter to the ATF that said, "ATF, all you tyrannical people will swing in the wind one day for your treasonous actions against the Constitution of the United States." With regard to the attack, McVeigh and his coconspirator, Terry Nichols, had been methodical. For months, McVeigh had scoped out various federal buildings that housed ATF and other law enforcement offices, finally settling on the Murrah building partly because he expected its glass front to shatter, making for a dramatic visual. His chosen date, of course, was no coincidence.

A searing debate ensued about the extent to which conservative propagandists and even some Republicans were culpable for the mind-set that led to the attack. *New York* magazine's cover for the week of May 8, 1995, blared "The Un-Americans," with photographs of Liddy, Oliver North, Rush Limbaugh, Pat Robertson, and two GOP senators, Phil Gramm and Jesse Helms. Conservatives pushed back hard. Gingrich, the man who had all but blamed the Democratic Party for a mentally ill mother's murder of her two kids, called any attempt to connect the dots between Republican rhetoric and the bombing "grotesque and offensive."

Four days after the bombing, Clinton went to Oklahoma City and delivered an uncharacteristically brief eulogy. The president who had been reduced to defending his relevance just a few days before now showed that he was relevant—as a son of the South (and a neighboring state, even) and as a Democrat trying to comfort a mostly Republican state, Clinton turned something of a corner with the speech. "You have lost too much," he told the mourners, "but you have not lost everything. And you have certainly not lost America, for we will stand with you for as many tomorrows as it takes."

American political discourse had once operated within broadly agreed-upon boundaries of self-restraint. It grew out of shared respect for our institutions; the shared experiences of Depression and world war that gave Democratic and Republican politicians a set of bonds that transcended partisan politics; and an understood need during the Cold War to be Americans at the end of the day. The Oklahoma tragedy allowed Clinton to feel and help forge that transcendence for a fleeting moment. But as he was learning and would learn even more pointedly later, those days were mostly gone.

. . .

For the first half of 1995, Clinton offered no budget or economic plan of his own, preferring to lambaste the deep spending cuts in the proposed Republican budget. Dick Morris, now fully back in the president's inner circle, persuaded him that he needed to put forward a plan of his own—he was, after all, the president. So on June 13, Clinton delivered an Oval Office address laying out his path toward eliminating the budget deficit in ten years. Gingrich and Dole had pledged to meet this goal in seven years. The deficit had already fallen by more than 40 percent under Clinton, from $290 billion in 1992 to $164 billion in 1995—largely as a result of the 1993 tax legislation and the improving economy—but deficit reduction was still a salient issue. Clinton told the country that the Republican cuts to education, entitlements, and the environment, and their tax cuts weighted toward the wealthy, were more than he could sign on to. But Clinton's ten-year timetable was also more than most liberal Democrats could sign on to, so he caught a lot of flak from his own party. But for the political purposes of this New Democrat president, whose first two years had gone down in conventional wisdom as "too liberal," this was just fine.

Thus the budget clash began in earnest. Over the summer of 1995, both sides issued repeated dire warnings to the public that if the other side didn't budge, the government might shut down. Most observers thought something so dysfunctional could never happen. For his part, Clinton had other things to worry about that summer, notably Bosnia—in July, the Bosnian Serb Army massacred eight thousand Bosnian Muslim men and boys at Srebrenica. The next month, Croatian forces massacred fourteen thousand Serbs in Krajina, precipitating the worst refugee crisis of the war. Clinton's national security adviser Anthony Lake had by this time persuaded reluctant European leaders to accept a more aggressive role, and NATO launched Operation Deliberate Force, flying some 3,500 sorties against Serb positions, which set the stage for the peace talks that would finally end the war. In September, Hillary went to Beijing to speak at a UN conference on women. Her speech, including the oft-cited line "Human rights are women's rights, and women's rights are human rights," spoken to a host country that was not known for sharing that view, quickly became regarded as one of her finest moments.

The fiscal year was set to end on September 30, 1995, and still there was no budget. Congress passed a continuing resolution to keep the lights on as the administration and Congress negotiated. But throughout October, talks went nowhere. Then, in another arena, tragedy struck. On November 4, Israeli prime minister Yitzhak Rabin was assassinated in Tel Aviv by a right-wing Jew enraged by Rabin's peacemaking efforts with the Palestinians. The assassination hit Clinton especially hard, because he and Rabin had grown to be close friends. "By the time he was killed," Clinton later wrote, "I had come to love him as I had rarely loved another man." The U.S. delegation to the funeral aboard Air Force One was bursting with ex-presidents, diplomats, senators, and House members, including Gingrich and Dole. The Republican leaders wanted some presidential face time on the return flight to talk budget, but White House aides shielded Clinton, writes John Harris, because they feared he would agree to terms "that would amount to a Republican victory." Instead, Clinton passed the time playing cards with *New York Daily News* publisher Mort Zuckerman.

The continuing resolution was set to expire at midnight on November 13. That day, Clinton summoned congressional leaders of both parties to the White House. He got into a heated discussion with Dick Armey, the House majority leader, over Medicare cuts. "Even if I drop to 5 percent in the polls," Clinton huffed, "if you want your budget, you'll have to get someone else to sit in this chair!" But the Republicans still held in their heads the image of Clinton as a president who could be rolled; they didn't believe he meant it.

This time, he did mean it. The new continuing resolution placed before him, to extend government operations a few more weeks, contained Medicare cuts that would have dramatically hiked premiums for senior citizens. Clinton vetoed it. And on November 14, nonessential operations of the federal government began shutting down.

At first, the shutdown hurt both parties in the eyes of the public, but then something big happened. Gingrich appeared at a newsmakers breakfast sponsored by the *Christian Science Monitor*. There, while being questioned about the shutdown by Lars-Erik Nelson, the widely respected Washington columnist for Zuckerman's *Daily News*, Gingrich launched into a harangue about how peeved he was not to have been able to talk about the budget with Clinton during the return flight from Tel Aviv. Then, displaying the utter lack of that internal governor that lets most politicians know when they should just shut up, he spoke of being forced to sit in the back of the plane and to exit through the rear.

The next day, the newspaper owned by the man who had enjoyed the president's company on that return flight produced one of the most memorable—and damaging—tabloid newspaper front pages of all time. "CRY BABY," the *Daily News* blared, in enormous bold type. Below the headline: "Newt's Tantrum: He closed down the government because Clinton made him sit at back of plane." Ed Murawinski's devastating cartoon showed a fleshy and corpulent Newt as a baby, bawling, stomping his feet, in diapers, clutching a baby bottle.

Gingrich later wrote that his remarks constituted the "single most avoidable mistake" he made as Speaker. He hustled to cut a deal to reopen the government on November 19, but by this point the Republicans were receiving far more blame for the shutdown than Clinton was. And that deal was temporary, too, so hard negotiating still had to be done.

The next round of talks began with Clinton making a key accommodation to the Republicans. On the same day the government reopened, he would publicly accept their seven-year deficit-reduction target. But he still didn't accept their budget cuts.

In the midst of the negotiations, the president went on an overseas trip, to Britain and Ireland, returning home in mid-December—just in time for a second government shutdown, which began on December 16. This one would last longer than the first, a full twenty-seven days. It was eased by the fact that roughly five hundred thousand federal employees were deemed "essential" and thus permitted to continue to come to work, but veterans' benefits, among other obligations, went unpaid that month.

After the holidays, polling showed the Republicans were paying a far higher political price for the impasse. Clinton had won. He managed to undo his reputation in Washington as someone who could be rolled; to the larger public, he'd stood his ground on some principles—opposing crippling cuts to entitlements, education, and the environment—on which a majority agreed with him. And he'd outstared Gingrich, who had simply miscalculated. "We made a mistake. We thought you would cave," he admitted to the president in early January 1996. It was a pretty good way to start a reelection year.

6

The Culture Wars

On the surface, life was fine in the America of 1996. The economy had rebounded, adding nearly 2.5 million jobs over the previous year. The Cold War was won, and the nation was at peace. Personal computers were suddenly and astonishingly connected to the outside world, and people could use them to chat with friends and family anywhere in the country or even beyond, or to do something called a "search" and learn in an instant the best bargain hotels in Paris or what season it was that Wilt Chamberlain averaged fifty points a game or which films were nominated for Best Picture in 1977. There were warnings from some pessimistic quarters that this new information age would alter our economy and our habits and even our brains in ways we couldn't possibly anticipate, but for most people the Internet was a miracle—the kind of miracle America naturally delivered to its citizens.

A bit below the surface, though, the United States *was* at war—with itself. This had started in the mid- to late 1980s, as the sweeping cultural changes that had their roots in the 1960s became more mainstream. Most Americans accepted these changes more or less ungrudgingly. But as the vast audiences created by Rush Limbaugh and his imitators had shown, many millions of Americans dissented from this transformation. They didn't like feminism and multiculturalism and diversity and gay people coming out of the closet, which started happening in fairly large numbers in the late 1980s, and they despised the way the media had (from their point of view) so casually embraced these changes, "shoving it down our throats" and enforcing this new blight called "political correctness."

In 1987, the University of Chicago philosopher Allan Bloom wrote *The Closing of the American Mind*, a broadside against the emergent enforced codes of speech and behavior on American campuses. It became a huge best seller. Bloom represented the high-end version of conservative dissent. Farther down the intellectual totem pole was a host of polemicists and provocateurs—Dinesh D'Souza and William Bennett between hard covers, and figures such as Morton Downey Jr. on television and Limbaugh and the others on radio—who kept the fire raging.

On those same college campuses, however, activists were impatient for far more change. Students—and many faculty, who had come up through the cultural studies departments of the 1970s—began scrutinizing textbooks and curricula, denouncing the dominance of the "dead white males" and arguing for more inclusive reading lists. "Hey hey, ho ho, Western Civ has got to go!" students at Stanford University chanted in 1988, with no less a figure than Jesse Jackson at their side. (They were objecting to a survey course called "Western Civilization," not the entire project of Western man, but still.) Some gay activists began "outing" closeted gay celebrities, trying to force them to be part of their movement. AIDS had taken a ghastly toll by this time, and the group ACT UP staged huge "kiss-ins" in front of St. Patrick's Cathedral. These and other matters were the fronts in "the culture wars," a phrase that seeped into general usage in the early 1990s.

As the first "first couple" to come from the Woodstock generation and not the Depression–World War II generation, the Clintons themselves constituted a front in these wars. This was particularly true of Hillary: she had, in fact, dabbled in radical politics when she was young (but only dabbled). Bill, with his mainstream political ambitions, had never really been drawn to that kind of activism. To their critics, mere facts like these didn't matter nearly as much as the overarching perception that the Clintons were somehow out to subvert the virtues that had sustained America through its era of abundance and dominance.

As candidate and president, Clinton had tried to split the culture war difference. On the one hand, he was a progressive-minded person whose worldview had been extensively shaped by his abhorrence of the casual racial discrimination he witnessed constantly as a child; beyond that he was an astute pol who saw the increasing voting power of women, African Americans, Latinos, and gay and lesbian voters. He therefore sought to be the leader of that coalition. On the other hand, as a New Democrat who had pledged to middle America that he would sand off all those "McGovernik" edges, he sought to sound more culturally conservative than Walter Mondale or Michael Dukakis had in the 1980s. And so it was that as a candidate he had pledged to make abortion "safe, legal, and rare." The "safe" and "legal" parts were intended to reassure the progressive coalition, while the "rare," which did, in fact, cause consternation among some pro-choice activists, was meant to signal to Americans outside the coalition that he bore them in mind, too—that his pro-choice position, while inevitable and necessary for a Democrat, was not meant to imply that he endorsed licentiousness.

This kind of straddling came naturally to Clinton as a matter of personality. Some presidents—Dwight Eisenhower and George W. Bush most notably—sought comparatively little information and made decisions quickly. Clinton was their opposite. He had an endless appetite for policy detail and could usually articulate the opposing position better than most of his actual foes. In the words of Joe Klein,

> Clinton's decision-making process was never truly complete until he had gone all the way and actually advocated— usually briefly, always privately—the opposite position from the one he would eventually take. This was difficult for even many of those closest to him to endure.

Clinton's equivocal style served him well at times—for example, when it came to negotiating a budget. But it did not suit the culture wars, on which battle lines were so resolutely drawn. After the 1994 midterm disaster, Clinton sought to put a little more distance between himself and cultural liberalism—he mused that perhaps school prayer, outlawed back in 1963, wasn't such a horrible idea. In August 1995, his Department of Education promulgated a few down-the-middle guidelines: organized prayer would still be banned, but private prayer groups and the carrying of Bibles would be permissible. The department also put forward a plan to let school districts legally impose policies requiring schoolchildren to wear uniforms.

A still-thornier issue was affirmative action, which had been initiated by Lyndon Johnson in 1965 and by the late 1980s was the target of a massive and well-organized conservative backlash. Gingrich and Dole had pledged that they would do all they could to destroy affirmative action and "racial quotas." In February 1995, Clinton had been speaking of affirmative action when he said that "we shouldn't be defending things that we can't defend." The administration then commenced a policy review; liberal groups waited nervously over the next few months, expecting that Clinton was going to cave.

He did not. Instead, in July, he gave a speech built around the ameliorative catchphrase "Mend it, don't end it." He defended government racial-preference programs and avowed that they would continue, while at the same time he promised to crack down on fraud in minority contracting, which was supposedly rife. Liberal and civil rights groups had so persuaded themselves that Clinton was going to ditch them that they accepted this quasi-compromise gladly.

On a third issue, Clinton was more resolute, and even courageous, as it was arguably the most fraught of the three. Intact dilation and extraction, or "partial-birth abortion" as it was rechristened by foes of abortion rights, involved the (usually) late termination of a pregnancy through means that were undeniably gruesome in their detail—in essence, a fetus's brain is suctioned out so that the skull collapses, allowing for easier extraction. Conservative opponents of abortion, always looking for an Achilles' heel to probe, had found a good one here; what person could possibly support such a procedure being conducted on a fetus that was in many cases close to fully formed?

The Republicans in Congress brought forward, in the fall of 1995, a ban on partial-birth abortions. It passed the House by a better than two-to-one margin and the Senate 54 to 44, with nine Democrats joining forty-five Republicans in support of the ban. Throughout that year and into the next, the year of Clinton's reelection, Republicans hammered at the issue as the political world awaited an announcement from the White House as to what Clinton's position would be.

That announcement came on April 10, 1996, when the president said that he would veto the ban. It was a tough day for Clinton; it was the same day he attended the memorial service for his close friend Ron Brown, the insider lawyer who had headed the Democratic National Committee in 1992 and was serving as secretary of commerce. Brown and several of his aides had died in a plane crash on a government mission to Croatia. On the abortion question, Clinton had closely studied the science, he writes in *My Life*, and learned that the procedure was "predominantly performed on women whose doctors had told them it was necessary to preserve their own lives or health," including their ability to bear children again. No one had demonstrated to him that the procedure was avoidable in these limited cases.

White House stagecraft around the veto included the presence at Clinton's side of five women who had undergone the procedure, three of whom thought of themselves as pro-life. But few were mollified; the House overrode his veto, while the Senate fell a few votes short. The veto stood, but Clinton knew it was lousy politics for him. And the Republicans weren't done with cultural politics yet.

• • •

Welfare reform was not a cultural issue per se; it was too weighed down by boring policy details. It nevertheless had its cultural aspects, because it was a proxy for race. Indeed, of all the subtle racial signals Clinton had sent to the white middle class in 1992, his pledge to "end welfare as we know it" was surely the central one. For a decade or more, conservatives had been pushing for welfare reform, advancing arguments against a status quo that they said was the epitome of the failure of big government. Many political scientists and economists had written extensively on the core need to move people from welfare to work, and other conservatives who had academic credentials but were polemicists more than scholars, notably Charles Murray, the author of the influential anti-welfare-state book *Losing Ground*, vituperated against the system ceaselessly.

They had a point. What had started as a modest program of relief for widows and orphans during the New Deal had morphed into an expansive set of benefits that offered perverse incentives to women: more money if they were single than married, and more money with each new child in the household, in most cases. Clinton had an intellectually honest desire to change that. And the fact that it was good politics didn't hurt.

But as long as the Democrats were running Congress, welfare reform wasn't going anywhere. Many Democrats recognized the problems in the system, but many others were distrustful, sometimes with good reason, of the motives of those who advocated "reform." Some conservatives did want the system to work better, but many others just wanted to slash spending and make poor people fend for themselves. Large majorities favored ending, in the oft-invoked phrase of the day, the "cycle of dependency." Welfare was the most prominent and controversial of a set of issues, which also included affirmative action and higher education standards, on which liberals were obliged to defend a hard-to-support status quo that deep down many knew wasn't working.

When Gingrich and the new Republican majority took over in January 1995, welfare reform was brought back on the table.

Clinton knew he had a campaign pledge to deliver on, so he was willing to deal. But there was a fundamental difference between his approach and that of the Republicans: Clinton, while aware that part of the point over the longer haul was to save the government money, believed that, in the near term, reform would require generous investments in work training and child care to help wean the most destitute Americans off the system. The Republicans wanted nothing to do with that—they just wanted to give none-too-generous block grants to the states and let them handle the matter however they saw fit. Clinton also wanted legal immigrants to be eligible, and Republicans firmly did not.

These and other differences led Clinton to veto the first two versions of welfare reform the Republican Congress sent him. Vetoing one of the measures, on January 9, 1996, Clinton said it was too punitive, especially toward the children of recipients. "The Congress should not use the words 'welfare reform' as a cover to violate the nation's values," he said. "We must demand responsibility from young mothers and young fathers, not penalize children for their parents' mistakes."

Even with the two vetoes, the Republicans had the upper hand, and they knew it: Clinton's 1992 pledge probably meant that he was going to have to sign something; pressure would surely mount as the election drew nearer. Republicans had miscalculated with respect to the government shutdown, but this time they got it right. They passed a third welfare reform bill in July 1996, and up it went, awaiting Clinton's signature.

Thus arrived one of the defining moments of Clinton's presidency. The new bill did constitute an improvement over the two earlier versions. It retained a federal guarantee of medical and food aid and actually increased federal childcare assistance by 40 percent over current levels. But it had nothing near the levels of support for transition-to-work programs that Clinton would have preferred, and it still gave states wide latitude to use their block grant money punitively if they desired, which many of them would eventually do. Moreover, the bill had passed both houses of Congress comfortably.

In the House, only 30 Democrats voted for it, while 165 opposed; but in the Senate, the Democrats were evenly split, 23 votes on each side. This was the context in which Clinton gathered his top aides and cabinet on the morning of Wednesday, July 31, 1996. He opened the meeting by asking simply, "What should we do?"

George Stephanopoulos wrote that the atmosphere at the meeting was "self-consciously statesmanlike, as if we were gathered for a council of war." The assembled took their turns. Most wanted Clinton to veto. Donna Shalala, the secretary of health and human services, argued strongly against the bill, as did labor secretary Robert Reich, chief of staff Leon Panetta, deputy chief of staff Harold Ickes, chief economic adviser Laura Tyson, and even the more centrist Treasury secretary Robert Rubin (who had replaced Lloyd Bentsen the previous year). Stephanopoulos was on this side as well.

Most of them made straight policy arguments; Stephanopoulos mixed in some politics, trying to persuade the president that he had taken other unpopular stands and survived those. Mickey Kantor, the U.S. trade representative, and political aide Rahm Emanuel wanted Clinton to sign. So did Bruce Reed, the president's chief domestic policy adviser and the aide most closely affiliated with the Democratic Leadership Council, which very much wanted Clinton to sign. Reed acknowledged the bill's many flaws, especially its exclusion of legal immigrants, but he argued that a third veto would break faith with the voters who had supported him expecting him to keep this promise.

The man who was perhaps the president's most influential adviser on the question wasn't present. Dick Morris had spent the summer warning Clinton that if he vetoed another welfare reform bill, he could lose the 1996 election. Morris's polling showed that signing the bill would rocket him to a fifteen-point lead over Bob Dole, who had secured the Republican nomination, whereas vetoing it would put the president in a three-point hole and give Dole a huge club to swing at Clinton all fall. Also not present was Hillary Clinton. It was common knowledge among this group that she wanted a veto, but the failure of health care and the continuing Whitewater grief—Ken Starr had actually hauled her down to a Washington courtroom to appear before a grand jury in the spring, ending the courtesy of visiting the White House to interview the Clintons—put her in a tough position. If the president vetoed the bill and suffered for it politically, she sure didn't want to be seen as the reason.

Clinton concluded the meeting taking no position, although aides could see that Reed's arguments seemed to sink in. The president's concluding comment was equivocal: "This is a decent welfare bill wrapped in a sack of shit." He then retreated to the Oval Office with Leon Panetta and Al Gore. The vice president had been the only one besides Clinton who had not expressed a view in the larger meeting, but now he told the president that he supported signing, arguing that Clinton would never have another chance to keep this central campaign promise. And that tipped things. Panetta sent word to Democrats on the Hill that Clinton would sign. The president went to the White House briefing to deliver the news to reporters himself. He would sign the most fundamental departure in federal poverty policy in six decades.

A furor ensued among liberals. Some high-level staff resigned in protest, among them Peter Edelman, a prominent poverty expert and the husband of Marian Wright Edelman, a longtime friend of Hillary's. Senator Daniel Patrick Moynihan, who had supported a milder welfare reform effort in the 1980s and who was regarded in Washington as a high authority on the subject, was furious. The previous fall, Moynihan had warned: "If this administration wants to go down in history as the one that abandoned, eagerly abandoned, the national commitment to children, so be it. I would not want to be associated with such an enterprise, and I shall not be. I cannot believe this is happening. It has never happened before." When Clinton signed the bill, he said simply: "The president has made his decision. Let us hope it is for the best."

. . .

The legacy of welfare reform is, of course, complex. The direst liberal predictions did not come true. In states that genuinely tried to move people to work with proper support, the results were tolerable and sometimes even good—caseloads declined, more than half of the mothers who left welfare found work, and child poverty went down. In other states, basic monthly benefits *were* slashed dramatically and have stayed that way. But the short-term political benefit was undeniable. Bob Dole had nothing, really, to run on.

In another situation, Dole might have been a more formidable candidate. A World War II hero who had lost the use of one arm from a battle injury, he was a rock-ribbed heartland conservative, without being radical. He faced no serious competition for the nomination. Only Steve Forbes, the multimillionaire publisher who had one issue (the flat tax), and Pat Buchanan, the paleo-conservative culture warrior, won primaries, but just a few—Dole took all but five contests. He had, so far as anyone knew, lived a life of integrity. His wife, Elizabeth, was an asset, too. She had been a cabinet secretary under both Ronald Reagan and George H. W. Bush, and during her time as secretary of transportation she had actually accomplished something—something visible to most Americans on a daily basis: she instituted the requirement of the brake light in every new car's rear windshield.

But after all the vexation in 1992 about whether the country was ready for a Woodstock generation president, it turned out that voters didn't want to go back to the generation that had fought in World War II. By 1996, *Seinfeld* and *The Simpsons* were part of the cultural furniture, and Dole seemed to have come from another America. At one sad point in late September, at a Los Angeles fundraiser, he mistakenly referred to the Los Angeles Dodgers as the "Brooklyn Dodgers"—the team had, of course, moved west in 1957.

Clinton had his problems, too. The Democratic National Convention was held in Chicago a month after he announced he'd sign the welfare bill. There was unrest afoot, and Jesse Jackson and Mario Cuomo criticized Clinton's decision from the podium. Clinton's own speech, laying out his agenda for a second term, was less than inspiring. He offered tax cuts and tax credits, more test-ing of students, a balanced budget. The president had started the year by saying, in his State of the Union address, that "the era of big government is over." Now he was filling in that picture. This was Morris's theory of "triangulation": that Clinton should keep his distance from some old-line liberal ideas, adopt and modify a few Republican ones, and exist as an independent third force separate from both parties.

Morris was out of the picture by the fall, having been felled by the revelation that he'd been regularly seeing a prostitute (and a dominatrix at that!), sometimes letting her listen in on the exten-sion as he talked with the president. But his ideas were alive and well. And it's hard to say, in pure electoral terms, that Morris was wrong. Signing the bill clearly made Clinton's political path easier, and besides, he did have genuine differences with the party's left wing. He had campaigned in 1992 emphasizing those differences, so papering over them in 1996 might have cost him support in the middle and would have constituted a reneging on some key cam-paign promises.

The Democratic ticket faced a fund-raising scandal that fall, around the allegation that the Democratic National Committee had accepted foreign campaign donations, but no smoking gun turned up. Ross Perot was running again as a third-party candidate, but this time, with the economy out of the doldrums and the deficit shrinking, he was a sideshow. Dole made a pretty shrewd vice presidential choice in Jack Kemp, the former congressman and secretary of housing and urban development, who was sin-cere in his belief that the Republican Party should do more to reach out to African American and poor voters. But still Dole could get no traction.

It was the lowest turnout for an election—just under 50 percent—since 1924, but once the votes were tabulated, Clin-ton had beaten Dole by about nine percentage points, and his victory in the electoral college was 379 to 159, even more impressive than his showing in 1992. The campaign-finance issue probably cost him a majority of the popular vote. He had sorely wanted that majority, but even so, he became the first Democrat to win reelection as president since Franklin Roosevelt. A lot of those Reagan Democrats who had left their party in 1980 had clearly come back. The Democrats were divided over some of the ways Clinton got there, but they couldn't argue with the result.

But the Republicans still controlled Congress, and there was little reason to think much legislation would get passed. In mid-January 1997, a few days before his second inauguration, Clinton met with aides at Blair House to sketch out his second-term agenda. Carl Cannon, a top White House correspondent, reported the result as "scaled-down expectations in domestic policy." The second term was looking as if it was going to be pretty uneventful.

7

Hitting His Stride

During his reelection campaign, Clinton used the rebounding economy as any incumbent president in his situation would. In his convention acceptance speech, he boasted of "ten million new jobs, over half of them high-wage jobs." He bragged about reducing the deficit, which had stood at a record $290 billion the year he was elected, down now by 60 percent. The economy certainly was a net plus for him, but even so, the recovery wasn't quite a political slam dunk. In Chicago during the final week of the campaign, Clinton talked up the economy, but his rhetoric was still decidedly cautious. "America's awake," he told his audience, "and moving in the right direction."

It didn't take long into the second term, though, to see that America had been doing something more than just waking up. The Dow Jones Industrial Average, which stood at 3,241 when Clinton took office, opened 1997 at 6,448, nearly doubled. Gains in 1995 and 1996 had been 33 and 26 percent, respectively, stratospheric numbers for the Dow. The NASDAQ exchange had also roughly doubled in value, from 696 to 1,380. (All these are nominal numbers, not adjusted for inflation.) The economy grew at a strong 3.8 percent in 1996, including an off-the-charts 7.2 percent for the second quarter. Median household incomes had gone up an enviable

7.3 percent during Clinton's first term—compared to a 5.4 percent *decline* during George H. W. Bush's four years.

Clinton and his supporters attributed all this to the 1993 budget, the one that passed by a single vote in each house of Congress. Specifically, they cited the decision to attack the budget deficit as the key decision that restored economic confidence. Conservatives argued, and have tried to argue ever since, that that is nonsense, and that Ronald Reagan had somehow made it all happen, years after leaving office. This partisan political quarrel will never be settled, but the fact is that, at the time, most voters were happy to give Clinton the bulk of the credit. As he opened his second term, his approval numbers sat just north of 60 percent.

There were signs aplenty in early 1997 that the economy was starting to roar. A leading factor had less to do with any policies that emanated from the White House than with the vast changes sweeping through the economy, namely the tech boom and what came to be called the "dot-com bubble." The commercial growth of the Internet, starting in 1995 but coming into fuller flower by 1997, led venture capitalists to make huge (and occasionally quite unwise) investments in new Internet start-ups, as new companies held lavish and Gatsbyesque launch parties, built eye-popping corporate campuses, and inaugurated the soon-to-be-familiar practices of looser work rules—foosball tables in the corporate rec room and so on—that marked them as definitely not your father's stodgy corporation. Glossy magazine articles, books, and movies glamorized these new hipster capitalists, and consumers were utterly amazed to find that a book could be ordered by tapping a few keys on their computers and then delivered right to their doorsteps. (Amazon.com began its online life in the summer of 1995, selling only books.)

It was one of those astonishing and rare moments in history: when we left one age and entered another, a new "information age" in which work and the economy—and play, too; oh, how play was transformed!—became driven by information stored on computers that could speak to other computers the world over. Social critics and theorists raised questions and doubts about what it meant to live in a "hyper-mediated" culture, and about the almost mystical fervor with which proponents greeted this new era. But the average person was quite comfortable with it all, and for capitalists it meant the potential for vast new riches made of money that hadn't even existed before.

All this good news made for an optimism that gave Clinton some political breathing room—and plenty of leverage. So when the president sat down to negotiate a budget with Newt Gingrich and Trent Lott of Mississippi—Bob Dole's successor as Senate majority leader—Gingrich didn't threaten any shutdowns, and Clinton no longer had to protest that he was still constitutionally relevant. The latest economic statistics reinforced this dynamic. Growth for the first quarter of 1997 came in at a gaudy 5.6 percent, and the deficit was now projected to drop to just $71 billion. In such a climate, there wasn't a lot the Republicans could do, and by May 2—absurdly early by the usual standards—Clinton and the Congress had reached a budget deal. The deal was history making in that the two sides agreed that by 2002 they would balance the budget—something that hadn't happened since 1969.

In the deal, the Republicans got a capital gains tax cut and Medicare and Medicaid savings totaling about $140 billion over five years. In return for his concessions, Clinton won new investments in children's health care, about $24 billion worth; an increase of $40 billion in higher-education spending; more money to urge businesses to hire welfare recipients; and restored health benefits for disabled legal immigrants, which the Republicans had eliminated in the previous year's welfare reform bill. These did not constitute a second coming of the New Deal, but they were enough for Senator Phil Gramm of Texas, an unrelenting Republican budget hawk, to complain that "the most permanent feature" of the deal was an increase in spending on social programs that "the president has rightly compared to the explosion of social spending that occurred in the 1960s." The best economic news was yet to come, although, perhaps inevitably, it wouldn't translate into harmonious relations with Congress.

. . .

Clinton got more good news as his second term began: in mid-February, Ken Starr, by now very clearly Clinton's nemesis, announced that he would soon resign as special prosecutor and become dean of the law school at Pepperdine University in Malibu, California. Starr had pursued the Clintons aggressively but had been mostly rolling snake eyes on a range of fronts. The previous August, his prosecutors had lost a crucial case against two small-time bankers in Arkansas based on charges that they had concealed certain actions they'd taken on behalf of Bill Clinton's 1990 gubernatorial campaign. The prosecutors obviously wanted to squeeze the two men, but the acquittals ended any hope of that. Starr had also hoped to get Susan McDougal, the ex-wife of Whitewater investor Jim McDougal, to turn on Clinton, even to say that she'd had an affair with the president. She would not, and as the price of her silence, she spent a total of nearly two years in prison, including eight months in solitary confinement, a portion of which was spent in a Plexiglas-enclosed soundproof cell. The ACLU of Southern California called her treatment "barbaric."

By 1997, some observers were beginning to wonder why Starr was still at it, but neither the setbacks nor the questions quieted the right-wing noise machine. Talk radio and conservative columnists, abetted by a small number of mainstream reporters at the *Washington Post*, the *New York Times*, NBC, and ABC who were heavily invested in the Whitewater story (and in the leaks they were almost certainly getting from Starr's prosecutors), kept banging the drums. They were joined by this time by the Fox News Channel, which had debuted during the 1996 campaign and was owned by Rupert Murdoch and headed by former Republican consultant Roger Ailes.

Murdoch and Ailes would become key figures in the get-Clinton campaign, but in the capital, the unquestioned drum major was William Safire, the former Nixon speechwriter turned *New York Times* columnist. Safire was respected in Washington high culture, even beloved; he had shown a willingness occasionally to use his perch to attack Republicans, so to establishment Washington the former Nixon spinmeister had a reputation as a straight shooter. But on Whitewater, on which Safire wrote column after column from the time the story broke, he was a propagandist. He produced an endless blizzard of columns alleging that the Clintons were probably guilty of all manner of criminal activity—in one column, for example, he wrote that events would likely soon prove that both Clintons were "accomplices in stealing $50,000 from the poor." (Events did not so prove.) In January 1996, he set Beltway tongues wagging by calling Hillary Clinton a "congenital liar." Thirteen months later, he wrote that "stunning indictments" on White-water and other matters were imminent.

Starr's announced departure would seemingly bring the whole scandal industry to an end. Sources close to Starr told journalists that his "major decision" before he left office during the summer would be "when and whether to announce that he will not seek prosecution of the Clintons." To most observers it seemed unlikely that a prosecutor who'd spent three years looking zealously for signs of wrongdoing would be quitting if he had the goods. It looked as if Starr was running up the white flag; the fact that he was moving three thousand miles to what was arguably America's most pictur-esque college campus in one of its most breathtaking locations—to a position funded, as it happened, by Richard Mellon Scaife, who had bankrolled the so-called Arkansas Project—only reinforced the image of a man who saw failure coming and wanted to get as psychically far away from Washington as possible.

The right-wing press flew into a rage at Starr. Safire led the charge, with a column headlined "The Big Flinch" that flayed Starr for his "warped view of duty" and advised that he "get out of town and let someone else finish the job he misled the nation he was pre-pared to do." Similar broadsides emanated from the *Wall Street*

Journal editorial page and other venues, and within a few frenzied days Starr reversed field and announced he'd be staying after all.

From that point the Whitewater news turned decidedly more sour for the White House. On April 22, 1997, a federal judge in Arkansas—who happened to have worked on the 1974 congressional campaign of John Paul Hammerschmidt, the Republican who'd defeated Clinton in his run for Congress—extended Starr's term for another six months after the prosecutor said publicly that he had evidence of "concealment and destruction of evidence and intimidation of witnesses." Three days later, a federal circuit court ordered the White House to turn over notes Starr had subpoenaed that had been taken by administration lawyers during prosecutors' examination of Hillary Clinton. In late May, the U.S. Supreme Court ruled that a sexual harassment suit filed by an Arkansas woman named Paula Jones, who alleged that Clinton had sexually assaulted her at a Little Rock hotel in 1991, could proceed. The court held, unanimously, that a sitting president had no right to temporary immunity from civil litigation aimed at him. Writing for the court, Justice John Paul Stevens, a liberal, argued that fighting Jones's lawsuit "appears to us highly unlikely to occupy any substantial amount of [the president's] time."

Stevens was assuming the existence of the postwar political order that he'd known all his adult life—where there was partisanship, certainly, but it just didn't go beyond a certain agreed-upon point. He probably assumed that the Jones lawsuit was one lonely woman's quest for justice, and he would surely have been shocked to know the truth of the matter—that by May 1997 there existed a cottage industry of conservative activists who were scheming to use Jones's allegations to bring Clinton down.

There were figures in Starr's office, such as Hickman Ewing, Starr's Little Rock–based prosecutor, and Paul Rosenzweig, who wrote legal briefs for Starr, who had decided that they were turning up nothing on Whitewater and needed to expand their probe into Clinton's personal life. There were Washington legal power couples Ted and Barbara Olson; federal appeals court judge Laurence

Silberman and his wife, Ricky; and husband-and-wife prosecutors Joseph DiGenova and Victoria Toensing, who worked either behind the scenes or in front of the TV cameras to see that both Bill and Hillary Clinton were laid low. There were lawyers in private practice, notably Jerome Marcus and George Conway, who were eager to play a role in discrediting Clinton as well. After 1994, when Jones filed her lawsuit, these lawyers had come to see the suit as the most likely vehicle through which they might get Clinton to commit perjury or otherwise obstruct justice by denying any of the many sexual liaisons of which he'd been accused. And, finally, there was Linda Tripp, a former Bush White House aide whom the Clinton team had disliked but retained, who had recently been transferred to the Pentagon (and given a raise to boot), but who was nursing her grudge.

. . .

When his presidency started, Clinton was hesitant in the realm of foreign affairs. Under the circumstances of 1992–93, this was, in a sense, acceptable to the voters. The Cold War had been won, Russia was no longer a threat, terrorism was not yet a direct menace; Bush had moved heaven and earth to make the 1992 campaign a referendum on foreign policy, and the voters had shrugged.

Clinton and the country quickly learned that the world still required American attention after all, but the new president seemed at times unsure of himself. He was criticized in general terms for "tactical ad-hockery" and lacking a grand strategic vision. On Bosnia, he was rebuked for delay, indecision, and too much deference to European leaders. His efforts stood as an improvement over the detachment of Bush and Baker, but at the same time, this was the greatest slaughter on European soil since World War II, and the American president appeared to be doing nothing. The *Black Hawk Down* episode in Mogadishu, while not Clinton's fault per se, didn't help his standing. His Haitian intervention on behalf of Aristide had not been popular. North Korea had moved toward nuclear weaponization, and the deal that Jimmy Carter had reached with Pyongyang was fragile; given the North's secrecy, no one could be completely sure whether the deal had taken or not.

As time went on, though, Clinton's confidence grew. There were some notable successes, by far the most important of which was the Dayton Agreement, reached in December 1995 under the leadership of chief negotiator Richard Holbrooke, which ended the Bosnian wars. The bloodshed stopped, the peace held, and one annex of the agreement still stands as the basic framework of the constitution of Bosnia and Herzegovina. Another courageous move, especially given Clinton's perceived draft-dodger history, was his normalization of relations with Vietnam, also in 1995. He had made tangible contributions to the British-Irish peace process, and the bond he had developed with Yitzhak Rabin deepened his belief that he could bring peace to the Middle East.

Another personal bond Clinton developed was with Russia's president, Boris Yeltsin. The first postcommunist, democratically elected president of the Russian Federation, Yeltsin was both brave (standing up to the Communists who had attempted a coup in 1991) and undisciplined (an excessive fondness for the bottle), both visionary and puerile. In part because Yeltsin, too, faced enormous domestic pressures from his right—factions enraged by the diminution of Russian power since 1989—Clinton felt a kinship with the Russian leader. In 1994, he'd invited Yeltsin to visit Franklin Roosevelt's estate, urging him there that the two should "prove the pundits wrong. They want to write about a big blow-up. Let's disappoint them."

And there were, to be sure, instances of cooperation. The United States took steps to help Russia make the transition to liberal democracy, such as providing funds to stabilize the economy and offering advice about the regulatory structures that would be needed. In 1994, the administration reached an important and complicated agreement with Russia, Ukraine, Kazakhstan, and Belarus with respect to the proper handling of nuclear material left over from the Soviet era. Yet there remained moments of conflict, and the long-held suspicions of this old enemy were now commingled with a sense of superiority because Russia was so much weaker than the USSR had been.

These two approaches—encouraging Russia to join the West on the one hand, while on the other bearing in mind that Russia still couldn't be thought of as exactly an ally—were in tension throughout the Clinton years, and both came to a head in the summer of 1997. At the summit of the Group of Seven nations that set the ground rules of the international economy, held in Denver on June 20–22, Russia was admitted as the eighth member, over a dinner of seared Colorado bison in whiskey and tortilla sauce. Yeltsin was delighted to see the G-7 become the G-8. And then, a mere two weeks later, Yeltsin was something other than delighted when NATO extended offers of membership to Poland, the Czech Republic, and Hungary.

The groundwork for this move had been laid in March, when Clinton and Yeltsin met in Helsinki for a summit. Here, Clinton's intuitive grasp of politics, and the pressures Yeltsin was facing at home, served him well. Yeltsin was deeply resistant to NATO expansion, and he wanted a commitment from Clinton that expansion would stop with the three nations under consideration. Clinton said he couldn't make such a commitment and that Yeltsin's best option was to say the move had his blessing. He offered Yeltsin a way to sell it at home:

> I pointed out that a declaration that NATO would stop its expansion with the Warsaw Pact nations would be tantamount to announcing a new dividing line in Europe, with a smaller Russian empire. That would make Russia look weaker, not stronger, whereas a NATO-Russia agreement would boost Russia's standing.

Yeltsin agreed, though he was nervous about his own right-wing domestic opponents—arguably more fearsome than Clinton's, always ready to prey on the collective Russian historical memory of humiliation. Like most presidents, Clinton didn't fully appreciate

the extent to which Hitler and even Napoleon still loomed over
the Russian foreign policy psyche.

• • •

The year 1997 also saw a major development in the administration's
relations with China, as Clinton hosted President Jiang Zemin in
Washington for meetings and a formal state dinner. As a candidate,
Clinton had—as all candidates do—torn into his predecessor for
coddling China and promised that he would get tough on China's
human rights abuses. As president, Clinton had—as all presidents
do—come to see that the reality was a bit more complicated. In
1995, China was still only the world's eighth-largest economy,
behind Italy and even Brazil, but its GDP had been growing at 14
and 15 percent per year, and jobs, especially in high-tech manufacturing, were moving to the country from America at an alarm-
ing pace. China had to be bargained with.

Hillary Clinton's human rights speech in Beijing in 1995 had
been about as aggressive an assault, albeit a merely rhetorical one,
as an American administration had made on China since the first
opening under Richard Nixon nearly a quarter century earlier. In
time, there were small military manifestations of conflict; in late
1995 and early 1996, after the White House allowed Taiwanese
president Lee Teng-hui to visit the United States, the People's
Republic responded by conducting military exercises in the Taiwan
Strait, and the Clinton administration sent an aircraft carrier into
the region, the first time the United States had done so in seventeen years. But the bulk of the administration's work on China centered on trade and economic issues. The big breakthrough on that
front was yet to come, but at their Washington meeting, Clinton
and Jiang announced a deal allowing the sale of nonweapon nuclear
technology by U.S. companies to China.

The other major foreign policy development of 1997 came with
the election in the United Kingdom of the man who was soon
regarded as Clinton's soul mate, Tony Blair, the new prime minister and the young and charismatic leader of the Labour Party. Like

Clinton, Blair had waved good-bye to the paleo-liberalism—actually, in Labour's case, paleo-socialism—that had been hanging around his party's neck since Margaret Thatcher's day, and he led what he called "New Labour" to a landslide win in the May 1997 parliamentary election. What came to be known as the "Third Way"—the political course between conservatism and old-style liberalism that Clinton had embraced in 1992—had gone global. As Sidney Blumenthal wrote: "Clinton felt that he himself was leading an international movement."

So things stood as 1998 dawned. The economy was thundering along—in early January, Clinton met with aides for their first-ever discussion about what to do with the expected budget surplus. The Republicans on Capitol Hill were comparatively tame. Violent crime was way down, mostly having to do with new policing strategies put in place by mayors such as New York's Rudy Giuliani, but also having to do with Clinton's crime bill and those 100,000 new cops. The administration had undertaken a domestic initiative on race relations that, even if it didn't accomplish much that was concrete, still offered up some national feel-good moments: in May 1997, Clinton apologized to the survivors of the notorious Tuskegee experiments on African American men whose syphilis was studied by the government but not treated.

Sure, there were still problems in the world. One can always count, for example, on the Middle East to provide that. After Rabin's assassination, Israeli voters had taken a turn to the right, electing Benjamin Netanyahu, the Likud leader, as prime minister. Clinton had begun to think that securing an Israeli-Palestinian peace would be a fine capstone to his presidency. And that's what he was doing on January 20, 1998: hosting Netanyahu at the White House and proposing a new West Bank plan to him, but otherwise enjoying high approval ratings and no big problems, when, suddenly, his presidency and his life nearly caved in.

8

That Woman

The murmurings started, strangely enough, on a Saturday night—a time when even in media-obsessed Washington not many people are following the news. It was January 17, 1998; that day, Clinton, in a first for a sitting president, had testified in the Paula Jones lawsuit, taking questions under oath from her lawyers for six hours, and returning to the White House, the *New York Times* reported, "to check on the Asian fiscal crisis and on a daylong staff meeting about his State of the Union speech later this month." That night, the Drudge Report, a conservative online news aggregation site, posted a headline:

**NEWSWEEK KILLS STORY ON WHITE HOUSE INTERN,
BLOCKBUSTER REPORT;**

**23-YEAR-OLD FORMER WHITE HOUSE INTERN,
SEX RELATIONSHIP WITH PRESIDENT**

There was, as yet, no story, just this salacious headline. The next day on ABC's *This Week*, Bill Kristol, now the editor of the *Weekly Standard*, made the first reference to it on national television. That night, Drudge posted the ex-intern's name: Monica Lewinsky.

Though fairly new, the Drudge Report at that point had already gained a following among Washington journalists, and its proprietor, Matt Drudge, was celebrated on the right and despised by the left. The year before, when Sidney Blumenthal left journalism to join the White House staff, Drudge had published an unfounded and false rumor about him, and Blumenthal had sued him for libel. (The case was settled.) In a different era, that might have finished off a highly partisan publication run by a man with no journalistic background. But the mores and folkways of Washington were such that Drudge's influence merely grew. When Drudge decided to elevate a story, complete with a graphic of a blaring siren, Washington journalists eagerly picked up on it, seduced by the power of this new medium to spread news and gossip at barely comprehensible speeds.

Sometimes, as in the Blumenthal case, what Drudge promoted was just untrue. Other times, it was factually true but an obvious partisan hit job and dismissible on those grounds. But with this mind-bending headline, it turned out, he was onto something.

In June 1995, Lewinsky, then twenty-one years old, had come to work at the White House as an unpaid intern on the staff of Leon Panetta, the president's chief of staff. Those who watched her noticed that on those occasions when interns got to meet the president, Monica usually somehow made it to the front of the line. She managed once to introduce herself to Clinton, as the two passed each other in a hallway.

Then, that November brought the first government shutdown. Since some White House staff had to stay home, interns like Lewinsky, who normally toiled in the Old Executive Office Building next door, were imported to the West Wing to answer phones. Thus it was that on the night of November 15, Lewinsky found herself alone with Clinton. She pulled up her dress, giving him a peek at her thong underwear. Matters proceeded as they often do in such cases. She performed oral sex on him, although he stopped her before he reached climax, and even managed to call two members of Congress during the encounter. Toward the end, Clinton flicked at the intern badge dangling from Lewinsky's neck. "This could be a problem," he said.

Two nights later, there was another encounter, when Lewinsky brought the president some pizza that had been delivered to the White House. Then nothing for six weeks, by which time Lewinsky had moved into a paid staff position in the White House Office of Legislative Affairs. There was a third assignation on the afternoon of New Year's Eve, three more encounters in January and February 1996 before the president ended the relationship on February 19, and a final moment of weakness on March 31. At that point a White House deputy who understood what was going on had Lewinsky transferred to the Pentagon—a move that would prove in some ways even more fateful than the affair itself.

Why did Clinton do it? It was unfathomably irresponsible. He knew what kind of enemies he had. He knew that Ken Starr and his deputies would overturn every stone they could to find something on him. He knew that reckless behavior on his part could imperil not just his presidency, but *the* presidency, as well as, potentially, Democratic and progressive politics for years. And still, he took the plunge. In *My Life*, he explained his weakness as an effort to lead the "parallel lives" that he had pursued since his childhood, a life of public joy and exuberance but no small amount of inner torment.

> I also came to understand that when I was exhausted, angry, or feeling isolated and alone, I was more vulnerable to making selfish and self-destructive personal mistakes about which I would later be ashamed. The current controversy was the latest casualty of my lifelong effort to lead parallel lives, to wall off my anger and grief and get on with my outer life, which I loved and lived well. During the government shutdowns I was engaged in two titanic struggles: a public one with Congress over the future of our country, and a private one to hold the old demons at bay. I had won the public fight and lost the private one.

In so doing, I had hurt more than my family and my administration. It was also damaging to the presidency and the American people. No matter how much pressure I was under, I should have been stronger and behaved better.

But he wasn't, and he didn't. It was by any measure selfish and out of control. And while it's hard to say whether this made it better or worse, the affair was not solely sexual: Clinton and Lewinsky had long phone calls, they shared things; he gave her a copy of Walt Whitman's *Leaves of Grass*, known for its celebration of things sensual, while she presented him with a copy of *Oy Vey! The Things They Say: A Book of Jewish Wit.*

When Lewinsky went to work at the Pentagon, she met Linda Tripp. Tripp disliked the Clintons intensely; she was a Republican, but beyond that she was upset at being transferred out of the White House. It was perhaps for that reason that she befriended Lewinsky, who had been similarly drummed out of the inner sanctum and shipped across the Potomac. If Lewinsky had been reassigned to the Interior Department or the Federal Aviation Administration, the whole thing might never have become public. But she wasn't, and she met Tripp. The two began talking; in time, Lewinsky started telling Tripp about the affair—angrily and in detail. Tripp started writing things down.

Meanwhile, Tripp had hired and befriended a literary agent, Lucianne Goldberg, hoping to sell a dishy book about Vince Foster. (She was one of the last people to see him alive.) Goldberg had a history as a conservative provocateur; she had once posed as a reporter on George McGovern's campaign while working for the Nixon team. Soon enough, Tripp was conveying the gist of Monica's story to Goldberg, who suggested to Tripp that she begin taping their phone calls. Tripp resisted at first, but Goldberg persuaded her that if the goal was to nail a sitting president on a sex scandal, hard proof would be vital: "Well, bubeleh, if you're going to go after the big kahuna, you better kill him."

And so, in early October 1997, Tripp began recording a series of confessional telephone chats—secretly and, indeed, illegally, since recording a conversation without informing the other party was a felony in Maryland, where Tripp lived. (Goldberg had assured her it would be legal.)

In the meantime, *Newsweek* investigative reporter Michael Isikoff had spent much of 1996 and 1997 writing various Clinton scandal stories, on Whitewater and on the allegation that Clinton and Gore had accepted illegal foreign donations during their reelection campaign. He had followed and written about the Paula Jones lawsuit from the beginning. But in mid-1997 he was pursuing a story about another woman, Kathleen Willey, who alleged that Clinton had groped her in the Oval Office in 1993. It was in the course of this pursuit that he met Tripp, who had supposedly seen Willey leave Clinton's office in a state of dishevelment. Tripp did not confirm Willey's account to Isikoff, but the two stayed in touch. It was also in mid-1997 that Isikoff had a chance encounter with the conservative polemicist Ann Coulter in the green room at CNBC. Coulter, Isikoff wrote later, "kept dropping hints suggesting inside knowledge about Jones's legal strategy. I remarked on this. Oh yes, she said with a laugh. 'There are lots of us busy elves working away in Santa's workshop.'" Isikoff tucked that away, and the next day called the conservative activist lawyer George Conway to learn more about what Coulter meant. Coulter, Conway, and others on the right were obsessed with Jones's lawsuit and the opportunity it presented to humiliate Clinton.

In October 1997, Tripp played her tape-recorded conversations with Lewinsky for Lucianne Goldberg for the first time. Goldberg then arranged for Tripp to meet Isikoff and play the tapes for him, but Isikoff refused—he felt, he wrote in his book on the scandal, that listening to tape recordings made without one party's consent went against the standards of journalism in which he was trained. Tripp and Goldberg kept working him, hoping that he would write a story in *Newsweek* that could potentially lead to a blockbuster book deal for Tripp: I was the president's girlfriend's confessor.

As these events were unfolding, the Jones lawsuit took a

conspiratorial turn. Back in 1994, Jones's charges had mostly served as fodder for late-night comics and supermarket tabloids. Then, in late 1996, Stuart Taylor Jr., a respected legal writer—albeit a staunchly conservative one—produced a lengthy article in the *American Lawyer* taking Jones's case seriously. Washington followed suit. Then came the Supreme Court ruling that her case could proceed while Clinton was president. Clinton offered to settle, for $700,000— but with no apology. Jones's lawyers urged her to take the money.

She heard them out, but by now Jones was listening to other people, too—conservatives who saw that her suit presented a chance to discredit or disgrace Clinton. She hired a new public relations person, Susan Carpenter-McMillan, a Los Angeles–based conservative activist who specialized in going on television and denouncing Clinton; the online magazine *Slate* called her a "first-class media hound, blessed with a savage wit, good looks, and—as one critic put it—'the tact of a bulldozer.'" In October 1997, the same month that Tripp first played Goldberg the tapes, Carpenter-McMillan urged Jones to refuse the settlement. She did, and, in exasperation, her two longtime attorneys quit the case. Jones hired new counsel from the Dallas law firm of Rader, Campbell, Fisher & Pyke. The firm had connections to a religious-right foundation, the Rutherford Institute, which agreed to help publicize and cover the costs of the suit. Rutherford had been created in 1982 to act as a sort of Christian civil liberties group; its main founder, John Whitehead, wrote a book that year, *The Second American Revolution*, arguing that the Bible should be the basis for all American law and decision making.

So things stood in the fall of 1997: over here, a politically motivated legal team, trying to find any sexual dirt it could on Clinton; over there, a similarly politically motivated group of people in possession of just such dirt. It didn't take long for their paths to cross. Jones's lawsuit was regularly in the news, so Tripp and Goldberg would have read of the new Rutherford association and would obviously have known that they were sitting on information that would be of keen interest to the Jones team. In fact, Tripp had *wanted* to be subpoenaed by Jones's lawyers—in that way, she would be going public with the Lewinsky details (laying the groundwork for her book deal) as a matter of legal compulsion and would feel less like she was betraying her friend. In November, Goldberg reached out on Tripp's behalf to Richard Porter, a lawyer—in fact, a partner of Starr's at Kirkland & Ellis—and former Republican opposition researcher who was part of the circle of "elves" who were working behind the scenes to help advance the Jones case. "After Goldberg finished telling Tripp's story," wrote the journalists Joe Conason and Gene Lyons, "Porter promised to take care of the subpoena."

Once that connection was made, the Jones lawyers knew the name *Lewinsky*. On December 5, 1997, they presented their witness list to the president's legal team. It included her name. Clinton's lawyers asked him about the nature of the relationship; he lied to them. The Jones lawyers subpoenaed Lewinsky. In a panic, she telephoned Clinton. Though their physical contact had long ago ended, the two had been talking regularly (and not always happily) because she was seeking to leave government and find a job in the private sector. Clinton had directed her toward his friend Vernon Jordan, a powerful and widely respected figure in the Washington legal community with a long history in civil rights, who would help her in her job search. Clinton told Lewinsky that if she filed an affidavit saying she had no information to contribute about Jones's allegations, she might avoid having to testify, and so she did it—stating that she and the president had never had sexual relations. She signed it on January 7, 1998.

Now that the Lewinsky group and the Jones lawyers had connected, all that remained was for them to find their way to Ken Starr. This happened at a restaurant in Philadelphia on January 8, when Porter, Jerome Marcus, and George Conway had dinner with Paul Rosenzweig of the independent counsel's office and told him the whole tale. The next day, Rosenzweig informed Jackie Bennett, a top prosecutor in Starr's office. After four years of snake eyes, the lucky prosecutor finally rolled a seven—finally had some evidence that could bring Clinton down.

Events moved quickly from there. On January 12, 1998, Starr directed Bennett to begin accepting information from Tripp, who had fired her old lawyer, a Democrat who was aghast that she had violated Maryland's taping laws, and hired the conservative attorney James Moody. On January 13, Tripp met with Lewinsky, this time wearing a wire supplied by Starr's office. On January 14, Moody played some of the (illegally recorded) Tripp-Lewinsky tapes for Conway and Coulter. On January 15, Bennett approached the Justice Department—specifically, Eric Holder, the deputy attorney general (and a future attorney general under Barack Obama)—to lay out the situation and to request authority to expand his faltering probe into the Lewinsky matter.

Referring to "inchoate criminality," Bennett told Holder that he suspected that Clinton and perhaps Jordan had urged Lewinsky to perjure herself. He had no actual evidence of this, but his office did gain possession of a so-called talking points memo written to Linda Tripp, coaching her on how to lie to prosecutors. The memo's authorship was unknown. If it had been written by Clinton or Vernon Jordan, that could be a crime. This charge raised the matter from mere extramarital sex to possible obstruction of justice. The Justice Department, fearful of exposing itself to charges that it was covering up for the president, granted permission.

On January 16, Tripp met Lewinsky again, at the food court at a northern Virginia mall called Pentagon City. But this time when Lewinsky showed up, she saw that Tripp had company—two FBI agents. "Ma'am," they told her, "you are in serious trouble. But we would like to give you an opportunity to save yourself." They led her to Room 1012 of the adjoining Ritz-Carlton hotel and questioned her for hours. When she asked to call her lawyer, they advised her not to. And on January 17, Clinton was deposed by Jones's lawyers—lying, again, as he had to his own lawyers the month before, on the rationalization that oral sex wasn't really sex. That was pure Clintonian parsing, a distinction that might hold sway in men's locker rooms but wouldn't do for a president.

Michael Isikoff was moving fast toward publishing a story in

Newsweek detailing some of these developments. The night before, Moody had allowed Isikoff and some colleagues to listen to one of Tripp's tapes. The next day was Saturday, the final deadline at a newsweekly that would hit newsstands on Monday morning. After an internal discussion that lasted the entire day, Isikoff's editors told him they wouldn't pull the trigger on something this explosive on such short notice; the story would not run. And that's when Conway and Goldberg tipped Matt Drudge, who posted that first Saturday night item.

· · ·

On Tuesday, January 20, Drudge posted a fuller story, explaining that Starr's office was in possession of "intimate taped conversations." Either directly or indirectly, Starr's office leaked information to two of its most reliable media conduits, Susan Schmidt of the *Washington Post* and Jackie Judd of ABC News. On Wednesday, the story officially broke in the mainstream press: "Clinton Accused of Urging Aide to Lie," screamed the banner headline in the *Post*. The most sensational allegation concerned "whether Clinton and his close friend Vernon Jordan encouraged a 24-year-old former White House intern to lie to lawyers for Paula Jones about whether the intern had an affair with the president." The story quoted anonymous sources as saying that prosecutors were in possession of a tape in which Lewinsky told Tripp that Clinton had instructed her to lie, and also to consult Jordan on what to say. And, of course, there was the talking points memo. If all this was true, it was quite plausibly—indeed almost surely—obstruction of justice and subornation of perjury, which would certainly be impeachable offenses.

The capital exploded in paroxysms of rage and revulsion. How *could* he? We knew he was kind of a cad, but this? An *intern*? In the Oval Office? Almost all the coverage, on television and in print, assumed the worst and assumed that all of it was true. "Starr Appears on Solid Ground" was a representative *Post* headline. No one in Washington in those first few days stopped to ask some obvious questions. Wasn't it rather Kafkaesque, the whole business—catching Clinton not having committed a serious crime, but telling someone to fib about a consensual affair, if he'd even done that? Wasn't it obvious that this was the result of a well-set "perjury trap" laid by a group of people who'd regarded Clinton as an illegitimate president since day one, going back to when Bob Dole declared in 1992 that Clinton had won no mandate? And perhaps most of all, if the leaks from Starr's office were highly unusual or even unethical, then how did we know about all this in the first place, and shouldn't someone be asking questions about Starr's tactics?

No time for any of that. The frenzy was on. There were predictions—such as the one put forward by ABC News commentator Sam Donaldson—that Clinton's presidency "could be numbered in days." George Stephanopoulos, now also with ABC News, mentioned the word *impeachment* on the air—a big deal coming from a former administration official, which gave others the license to use it as well.

Meanwhile, inside the White House, Clinton denied the story, and everyone wanted to believe him. He denied it to his family, his staff, his cabinet, his fellow Democrats, and the nation, although not as firmly as his supporters would have wanted. As fate would have it the president had three television interviews scheduled for that very day, originally planned to set the tone for his State of the Union address the following week. The first of these was with Jim Lehrer of PBS, who ditched his State of the Union questions and went straight to the matter at hand.

Lehrer: You had no sexual relationship with this young woman?

Clinton: There is not a sexual relationship; that is accurate.

"Is." Hmmm. In the two subsequent interviews, he shifted to the past tense, which reassured his staff and supporters, but everyone made a mental note. More parsing.

Meanwhile, the man was president of the United States. He had work to do—he hosted Netanyahu the day the scandal was breaking, and Yasser Arafat the next day. He also had ceremonial duties to perform. On the schedule for the night of January 21: a black-tie dinner for donors to the White House Preservation Society. This group included Richard Mellon Scaife; incredibly, the money man behind the Arkansas Project, which arguably was where all this had started in the first place, was a guest of the president on the very night the Lewinsky story broke. Hillary Clinton recalled in her autobiography, *Living History*, that "as the military aide announced his name and a White House photographer prepared to snap his picture, I realized it was Richard Mellon Scaife. . . . I greeted him as I would any guest in a receiving line," as did the president, but it had to be a surreal moment.

The week after the scandal broke was unlike any Washington had seen before. Clinton repeated and strengthened his denials. Starr subpoenaed a raft of White House aides and records. Lewinsky's attorney, William Ginsburg, who instantly became a ubiquitous television presence, negotiated privately (and publicly) for an immunity deal for his client. Clinton directed deputy chief of staff Harold Ickes and former secretary of commerce Mickey Kantor to run the White House's Lewinsky scandal response. James Carville vowed to wage "a war" over Starr's "skuzzy, slimy tactics."

On January 26, Clinton issued his most declarative denial yet, at the end of an event at which he'd been trying to talk about day care, class size, and education standards: "I want to say one thing to the American people. I want you to listen to me. I'm going to say this again. I did not have sexual relations with that woman, Miss Lewinsky. I never told anybody to lie, not a single time—never. These allegations are false. And I need to go back to work for the American people. Thank you."

The next morning, Hillary Clinton appeared on the *Today* show. Of course, she said, I believe my husband. And she went further: "This is the great story here, for anybody who is willing to find it and write about it and explain it, this vast right-wing conspiracy that has been conspiring against my husband since the day he announced for president." The phrase *vast right-wing conspiracy* caught on immediately, but not in the way Hillary Clinton hoped. Instead she was widely mocked, and the phrase became a punch line. Very few people, even among Washington journalists, knew the backstory on the relationships that had brought together Starr's office, Jones's lawyers, and the elves. Many who did know dismissed it. And in any case, many observers sniffed, no conspiracy had forced Bill Clinton to accept sexual favors from an intern. (Lewinsky was actually a full-time staffer during most of the liaison, but *intern* made it so much more scandalous, and the term was true enough, as that had been Lewinsky's status when the dalliance began.)

Clinton hoped, somehow, that he could bluff his way through this. But at the same time he knew what he had said to Jones's lawyers on January 17. He had squabbled relentlessly with them over the definition of the phrase *sexual relations*, said he couldn't recall whether he'd ever been alone with Lewinsky, and committed numerous other evasions. He hoped against hope that his deposition would never see the light of day. It's impossible to imagine how he carried on, knowing that he was lying and that he almost surely would be caught out one day—and still having to be the president of the United States. Talk about parallel lives!

But there was one thought he never entertained seriously: resigning. Even some supporters of his and critics of Starr wondered aloud if he shouldn't resign simply out of shame, for having sullied the people's house in such a way, assuming the charges were true. He was having none of it. He may have behaved indefensibly on a personal level, but he wasn't going to let his personal lapse be converted into political defeat. He certainly was not going to hand his political opponents his own scalp.

After the story broke, I called [lawyer] David Kendall and assured him that I had not suborned perjury or obstructed justice. It was clear to both of us that Starr was trying to create a firestorm to force me from office. He was off to a flying start, but I thought that if I could survive the public pounding for two weeks, the smoke would begin to clear, and the press and the public would focus on Starr's tactics, and a more balanced view of the matter would emerge. I knew I had made a terrible mistake, and I was determined not to compound it by allowing Starr to drive me from office. For now, the hysteria was overwhelming.

It certainly was. Every day brought new revelations, most of them false. In one notorious episode, the *Wall Street Journal* published a story on February 4, 1998, claiming that the president's steward, a man named Bayani Nelvis, had told Starr's grand jury that he'd seen Clinton and Lewinsky alone in the president's private study and had gone in afterward and picked up tissues with lipstick and "other stains." One of the story's authors was on television within minutes of the story going up on the paper's Web site. Washington was going nuts over it. But nothing about it was true. Nelvis had testified, that much was factual, but he'd said none of the things the *Journal* claimed. One of the story's reporters had asked the White House for comment, giving press secretary Joe Lockhart thirty minutes to respond. But the reporter called Lockhart back within minutes to say the story was up; there would be no response. Such was the atmosphere.

• • •

Just six days after the scandal broke, Clinton delivered his State of the Union address. The big question: would he address the scandal? Many commentators thought he had to, and indeed it seemed well nigh impossible that he could ignore not an elephant in the living room but a raging Tyrannosaurus. The notion was discussed in the White House but quickly dismissed. No, Clinton and his aides agreed, just go on being president. And thus was fashioned one of the strangest moments in American political history. All the pomp and ceremony of a State of the Union address—the overlong applause, the glad-handing as the president walked down the aisle, the inevitable insistence that "the state of our union is strong," met by the equally inevitable sustained applause from Democrats— continued as if the scandal didn't even exist. This, even as half the room, the Republicans, sneered contemptuously at him, and even as many or most pundits believed that Clinton might not be president for much more than another week.

But it was a lesson in the power of the office—he was still the president, and as much as critics might curse him on television, in his presence custom demanded that they still treat him like the president. And so he used the speech to boast about erasing the deficit: "Tonight, I come before you to announce that the federal deficit, once so incomprehensibly large that it had eleven zeros, will be simply zero," he said. He then shared his conclusion about what to do with the budget surplus: "Save Social Security first."

After those first couple of weeks, the clamor subsided a little, just as Clinton had hoped. It became clear that he was not going to resign, and the White House and its allies found their footing and started turning their guns on Starr. And a funny thing happened: Clinton's numbers went up, while Starr's plummeted. The president's approval rating had risen to 73 percent by early March, while Starr's was an anorexic 11 percent. Around this time, portions of Clinton's deposition were leaked and some of Clinton's evasions revealed, but they didn't move the needle. The American public had clearly decided that Clinton was a good president who had rescued the economy and, even if he did diddle around with this intern, they didn't exactly approve of course but it simply wasn't a high crime or misdemeanor warranting his removal from office. This was quite at odds with the views of Republicans and Beltway arbiters of conventional wisdom such as the *Washington Post*'s David Broder, the *New York Times*' Maureen Dowd, and NBC's Tim Russert. They were now in the position of pursuing a "truth" that the American people had already decided they didn't care about.

Over the course of the spring, Clinton turned some of his attention to foreign affairs. On St. Patrick's Day, he met again with

Gerry Adams and David Trimble, the Blair government's first minister for Northern Ireland, to nudge the parties to that conflict
toward peace. The nudging bore fruit a month later, when the Good
Friday Agreement was signed in Belfast, ending the historic conflict between Catholics and Protestants. Clinton wasn't present for
the signing, but he was in constant contact with all the parties via
telephone, and he called it "one of the happiest days of my presidency." Also in March, the president and First Lady flew to Africa
for an extended trip that highlighted American development
assistance and efforts on AIDS. They went to South Africa, where
President Nelson Mandela showed them around Robben Island
prison, which Mandela had involuntarily called home for twenty-
seven years. Clinton asked Mandela how he got over hating his
jailers; in fact, he had invited them to his inauguration. Mandela
described his thought process: "They have had me for twenty-
seven years. If I keep hating them, they will still have me. I wanted
to be free, and so I let it go." Mandela looked at Clinton heavily;
the president did not miss the point.

Also that spring, the administration began work to confront a
threat that was relatively new to the United States. The first terrorist bombing of New York's World Trade Center had taken place
in February 1993, but because it didn't do anywhere near the
amount of damage that was intended, it didn't register in the collective American consciousness with the gravity it might have.
Then, in March 1995, members of a Japanese terrorist cult group
released sarin gas in the Tokyo subway system, killing a dozen and
injuring fifty. And in June 1996, Islamic fundamentalist terrorists
detonated a truck bomb near a U.S. Air Force housing complex in
Khobar, Saudi Arabia, killing nineteen airmen. Through all this
time, U.S. intelligence agencies were tracking a surge in the number of terrorist training camps in the Middle East, and in jihadist
rhetoric that targeted America and especially its military bases on
Arab land.

In May 1998, Clinton used his commencement address to
midshipmen at the U.S. Naval Academy to boast that the federal

government had broken up terror rings planning attacks on New York's Holland Tunnel, the United Nations, and "our airlines," and to lay out a comprehensive anti-terror strategy. He created a national counterterrorism coordinator, naming to the position Richard Clarke, who would later gain attention as a major critic of George W. Bush's post–9/11 policies.

As summer arrived, more foreign policy: a lengthy trip to China, where Clinton again jousted with Jiang Zemin over human rights and intellectual property rights, among other issues. And Slobodan Milosevic reentered the picture. Bosnia had been quieted, but now an armed guerrilla group in Kosovo called the Kosovo Liberation Army (KLA), consisting of ethnic Albanians who wanted to leave Yugoslavia and be incorporated into a greater Albania, began launching attacks on Serbian installations in Kosovo. Milosevic responded with force, and fighting escalated over the spring and summer. Clinton dispatched Richard Holbrooke to the region in July, and Holbrooke read Milosevic the riot act and created an international stir by allowing himself to be photographed with members of the KLA, which another U.S. envoy had labeled a terrorist organization some months before.

Then, in August, Richard Clarke suddenly found himself a much busier man than he'd expected to be. On August 7, 1998, terrorist bombs tore through two U.S. embassies—in Dar es Salaam, Tanzania, and Nairobi, Kenya—killing more than 250 people. The original *New York Times* dispatch on the bombings suggested that the perpetrators might have been "a previously unknown group called the Liberation Army of the Islamic Sanctuaries." But in short order, suspicion centered on a man whose name was known to intelligence officials but not yet to the wider American public: Osama bin Laden.

Back in 1994, U.S. intelligence analysts believed that bin Laden, a Saudi national born to immense wealth, was financing at least three terrorist training camps in Sudan. The next year, he set up more camps in Yemen. In 1996, reacting to pressure from the United States and Saudi Arabia, Sudan expelled bin Laden, who moved to Afghanistan, where the extremist Taliban government gave him sanctuary. In 1997, a U.S.-backed multilateral mercenary force tried to abduct or kill bin Laden but failed. In early 1998, he issued a statement that because of America's military presence on Arab soil, Muslims should kill Americans, even civilians, anywhere in the world. And now came the embassy bombings, which the FBI and CIA confirmed to Clinton were carried out by bin Laden's group, al-Qaeda ("The Base").

Meanwhile, the Lewinsky scandal was still dominating the cable channels, even if the action had now largely moved behind closed doors. A parade of Clinton administration officials was called to testify before Starr's grand jury over the course of the spring and summer—Harold Ickes, Sidney Blumenthal, Bruce Lindsey, secretary Betty Currie, Secret Service agent Larry Cockell, and many others; most testified numerous times, emerging with the legal bills to prove it. Then, finally, on July 26, Starr subpoenaed the president himself to appear before his grand jury. This represented a new stage in the controversy: now, instead of just squeezing aides, Starr and his prosecutors would get to question Clinton himself directly. Clinton did not want the historical record to reflect that a president had been compelled to testify, so he agreed to do so voluntarily. The date was set for August 17. Clinton knew he was about to be asked specific questions under oath that he'd never been asked before. An already impossibly bizarre saga was about to become more so.

· · ·

On Saturday morning, August 15, 1998, Bill Clinton woke up his wife and told her the truth. He said he was ashamed and sorry, but he couldn't tell anyone, even her, at the time, because he didn't want "to be run out of office in the flood tide that followed my deposition in January." Then he told his daughter. The fates might have decided to hand the president an easier day, workwise, but there was a terrorist attack in Northern Ireland, a car bomb that killed twenty-eight people.

On the fateful day of the deposition, speechwriter Michael Waldman later wrote, the West Wing was "ghostly"; outside, "it was unnaturally dark, with rain pelting the windows," as if "a rather uncreative B-movie director had scripted the weather." Starr's prosecutors came to the Map Room of the White House; the grand jury, impaneled about ten blocks away, watched via video. When asked whether he was "physically intimate" with Monica Lewinsky, Clinton read a statement acknowledging conduct that was wrong but that stopped short of intercourse and thus didn't constitute "sexual relations" as he had understood the meaning of the term on January 17. The questioning continued for four hours. Clinton said he never asked anyone to lie. The whole thing wrapped up around 6:30 p.m.

White House staff had agreed in advance that Clinton would have to address the nation that night. Two speeches were prepared, one that expressed only contrition, and another that did that but added a few whacks at Starr and his tactics. Top aides argued that Clinton should just go full contrition. A stone-faced Hillary told him, "You're the one who got yourself into this mess, and only you can decide what to say about it." Clinton was still peeved, so, speaking from the same Map Room in which he'd been questioned, he went with the angry version. "Indeed," he owned up, "I did have a relationship with Miss Lewinsky that was not appropriate." Then he pivoted.

> This has gone on too long, cost too much, and hurt too many innocent people. Now, this matter is between me, the two people I love most—my wife and my daughter—and our God. I must put it right. . . . But it is private, and I intend to reclaim my family life for my family. It's nobody's business but ours. Even presidents have private lives.

The polls suggested that most Americans would have agreed, but that night Clinton was savaged by the pundits, who wanted contrition only. The next day, the first family left for their long-planned summer vacation on Martha's Vineyard. The news cameras lingered on the Clintons' backs as they walked across the White House lawn toward Marine One, Hillary on the left, Bill on the right, and Chelsea between them, holding both parents' hands. With his other hand, the president held the leash of his new dog, the well-named Buddy. At least, it was observed, he had one friend in the picture.

9

Unbreakable

It was August 18, 1998, the day the Clintons left for the Vineyard. It was not, to put it mildly, a joyous time. The president slept on the couch. August 19 was, of all complicating things, his birthday. There wasn't much celebrating.

But Clinton now had something else on his mind, aside from the scandal and his family's seething disapproval. Military commanders had located targets for the United States to strike back against Osama bin Laden. There were terrorist camps in Afghanistan, where bin Laden had moved after being expelled from Sudan in 1996, and two targets in Sudan, a tannery in which bin Laden had an interest and a chemical plant that the CIA suspected was being used to produce and/or store nerve gas.

And so, just days after the national humiliation of having to go on television to confess that he'd lied about Lewinsky, the president left his vacation, flew back to the White House, and announced to his countrymen that he had ordered a bombing raid on the above targets. It seemed to nearly everyone that Clinton had ordered the strikes to divert attention from the scandal. As fate would have it, Hollywood had even provided the script. The year before, the Barry Levinson film *Wag the Dog* was released, whose plot was based on such a scenario—a president embroiled in a sex scandal and seeking to change the subject by launching a war against Albania.

In truth, the Joint Chiefs of Staff, which approves such missions, would never consent to carrying out a military operation for the sake of saving a president's domestic hide; and further, the timing of such missions depends on factors ranging from the possession of hard knowledge about the target's whereabouts to considerations such as the weather and the prevailing winds. This did not stop most pundits and many Republicans from engaging in knee-slapping sport at Clinton's expense, although higher-level figures refrained. Newt Gingrich, who earlier in the year had said to Clinton's face, "Mr. President, we are going to run you out of town," now said, "I think the president did exactly the right thing today."

He did—and he didn't, in that the intelligence wasn't completely right and the strikes weren't successful. Bin Laden had fled the training camp where the CIA thought he was; the strikes missed him only by a matter of hours. Far more controversial, even putting the *Wag the Dog* scenario to the side, was the bombing of the chemical plant; critics said it was not clear that the plant had anything to do with terrorism. Some said the factory produced aspirin. A year later, after an exhaustive investigation, the *New York Times* found that the truth of the matter, as usual, was complicated. CIA director George Tenet and others had warned that the plant could be linked to bin Laden only by inference, while other officials, led by the national security adviser Sandy Berger, argued that the plant was a legitimate target and more terrorist strikes were in the planning stages. The administration, in Berger's words, "would have been derelict in our duty not to have proceeded." Whatever the doubts, two-thirds of Americans supported the strikes, and 61 percent said they considered Clinton to be a "credible military leader."

The president returned to the Vineyard, where there was the slightest of thaws in the marital chill, only to the extent that Bill and Hillary socialized together without evident rancor. Returning to Washington, Clinton faced a roiling Asian financial crisis that had now hit Russia, which defaulted on its foreign debt. Clinton

(with Hillary) made a quick trip to Russia to meet with Boris Yeltsin and assure him that more International Monetary Fund dollars
were on the way, and to Northern Ireland to advance the imple-
mentation of the Good Friday Agreement. While Clinton was
overseas, Senator Joseph Lieberman of Connecticut, a Democrat,
sharply attacked the president in exactly the kinds of moral terms
the pundits yearned to hear. The president's behavior, Lieberman
said on the Senate floor, "is not just inappropriate. It is immoral."

The scandal was, in one sense, winding down—the country certainly wanted to move on. But in another sense it was just heating
up, because establishment Washington didn't want to move on at
all, and, more important, neither did Ken Starr. When he announced
that he would be releasing a report on the entire matter, most
people assumed it would be a pretty standard-issue government
report.

What instead emerged—delivered to Congress on September 9,
1998, released to the broader public on September 11—was a
door-stopping 445-page report that accused Clinton of eleven
impeachable offenses and laid out every graphic sexual detail of
the Clinton-Lewinsky dalliance. There were discussions of the
presidential penis, of when he had and had not ejaculated, of an
episode when the president inserted a cigar into Lewinsky's vagina
and then licked it, saying, "It tastes good." The word *sex* (or some
variation thereof) appeared 581 times; the word *Whitewater* four
times. There was, of course, no public-interest need for all this
detail, and its purposes were clearly to humiliate the president and
to stoke public revulsion at his behavior. The report was initially
made available to journalists and other insiders by the Government
Printing Office, but soon enough it was published in book form and
became a best seller. It was even translated into several languages.

Starr appeared before a joint congressional committee to discuss the report, basking in the sycophantic questions from Republicans and deflecting the Democrats' irate ones. On the day of the
report's public release, Clinton was obliged to speak at the National

Prayer Breakfast, an event held annually in Washington since Dwight Eisenhower's day, and he used the occasion to apologize to Lewinsky and the nation.

> I don't think there is a fancy way to say that I have sinned. It is important to me that everybody who has been hurt know that the sorrow I feel is genuine—first and most important, my family, also my friends, my staff, my cabinet, Monica Lewinsky and her family, and the American people.
>
> I have asked all for their forgiveness. But I believe that to be forgiven, more than sorrow is required. At least two more things: First, genuine repentance, a determination to change and to repair breaches of my own making. I have repented.

The hysteria, which had quieted a bit, mounted again and reached an even higher pitch. More than fifty House members, a couple of Democrats among them, called on Clinton to resign, as did four senators. The talking heads again became screaming heads. And leading the media charge was not the *Wall Street Journal* or some other conservative newspaper, but the *New York Times*. The *Times*' editorial page editor, Howell Raines, had been thundering away about Clinton's depravity for months, although the editorial page of the nation's leading liberal newspaper stopped short of demanding the president's resignation. Raines worked himself into rages of such ferocity that he couldn't even recognize the presence in his prose of a glaring misplaced modifier as he congratulated Starr on laying bare the president's degeneracy: "Until it was measured by Kenneth Starr, no citizen—indeed, perhaps no member of his own family—could have grasped the completeness of President Clinton's mendacity or the magnitude of his recklessness." William Safire's feral columns, as well as those of Maureen Dowd and Frank Rich, who were counted as liberals in the taxonomy of A-level punditry but inveighed regularly against Clinton, completed a kind of anti-Clinton quadrifecta at the *Times*; only one columnist, Anthony Lewis, trained his fire chiefly on Starr.

The House Judiciary Committee, chaired by Illinois conservative Henry Hyde, moved to release the videotape of Clinton's testimony to Starr, so that all of America could see for itself the manner of man occupying their great and sacred house. The House Rules Committee set in motion the process that would lead to votes on articles of impeachment. But the videotape changed nothing, and two-thirds of Americans continued to oppose impeachment. James Carville ratcheted up his war on Starr, delivering scathing broadsides on the Sunday talk shows, and liberal groups and unions paid for television ads attacking Starr and defending the president. On October 8, 1998, the House of Representatives voted for just the third time in its history to open an impeachment inquiry against a president. No Republicans opposed the resolution, and thirty-one Democrats joined them in voting to move forward. The vote was 258 to 176.

The resolution called for an unlimited inquiry, as the Democratic House had done with respect to Richard Nixon in 1974. Indeed, privately, many Republicans saw this as revenge for Nixon—you got one of ours, so we're finally getting one of yours. But that is not, of course, what they said publicly. The proper public posture was to insist that they were acting with regret, even sadness, but that the imperative of getting to the truth placed this grim responsibility on their reluctant shoulders. The *New York Times* assayed Hyde's floor speech thus:

> Representative Hyde sought to strike a lofty tone in opening the Republicans' side of the hearing by saying, "Today we will vote on an historic resolution to begin an inquiry into whether the president has committed impeachable offenses."
>
> Every member, he said, was pulled in different questions [sic] "by many competing forces, but mostly we're moved by our consciences. We must listen to that still, small voice that whispers in our ear, 'Duty, duty, duty.'"
>
> This duty, he added, later in the debate, is "an onerous, miserable, rotten duty, but we have to do it."

Hyde's duty had been rendered more complicated by the revelation just after the Starr report came out that he—one of Clinton's
leading critics—had had an extramarital affair of his own some
years before. This story, too, became a huge controversy within
the controversy because of accusations that the White House
had leaked the story. Hyde at least 'fessed up, trying to explain
it away as a "youthful indiscretion," even though the affair had
begun when he was forty-one years old. The contention that forty-
one was considered "youthful" was not the only distortion of reality that was going on.

• • •

Meanwhile, the 1998 midterm election was barely a month away.
The Republicans held a 228–206 numerical advantage in the House,
and a ten-seat margin in the Senate. It has generally been the case
that midterm elections favor the party opposing the incumbent
president, and this pattern is most pronounced in the sixth year of
a presidency. Under these circumstances, it was expected that the
Republicans would augment their majorities, and probably by a considerable amount. Rarely in politics had anything been so obvious.

Conventional wisdom in Washington was that voters were going
to punish Democratic candidates across the country for the president's louche behavior. Gingrich spent the fall boasting that he
foresaw his Republicans gaining as many as forty House seats,
which would have given them a massive advantage. The history certainly said so—turnout normally favors Republicans in off-year
elections, because some groups that are strongly Democratic (blacks,
Latinos, young people) have a record of voting less heavily than they
do in presidential years. The universal assumption was that Democratic base voters would be demoralized and stay home, while
their Republican counterparts would be energized to do their small
part in sealing Clinton's fate.

There was still a nation and a world to attend to. In mid-October,
Clinton brought Israeli prime minister Benjamin Netanyahu and
Palestinian leader Yasser Arafat to a conference center on the Wye

River, on the Chesapeake Bay, in an effort to revive peace negotiations. The purpose of the meeting was to get the two sides to agree to a memorandum enforcing the so-called Oslo II Agreement on the status of the occupied territories, the West Bank and the Gaza Strip. The airport and seaport in Gaza and secure passage for Palestinians between Gaza and the West Bank were the easy parts. The sticking points centered on the number and type of Palestinian prisoners Israel would agree to release, and Netanyahu's insistence that the United States release from prison the convicted Israeli spy Jonathan Pollard, a move adamantly opposed by the Clinton administration's national security brain trust. The talks nearly collapsed several times. Clinton pushed the two leaders hard, keeping everyone up and talking with one another for nearly forty hours straight. The memorandum was signed on a Friday afternoon, shortly before the Jewish Sabbath; the parties rushed back to the White House to hold a press conference before sundown.

Meanwhile, the midterm campaign continued. Clinton did make some appearances—it wasn't the case that no Democrat wanted him around, because by now the pro-Clinton backlash among Democrats and liberals was considerable. People who'd never supported him or had been lukewarm because of his more centrist positions now decided that what was at stake here was not Clinton's merits or demerits, but what they saw in effect as a constitutionalized coup d'état.

Even so, Bill Clinton was not the star Democratic attraction on the campaign trail that fall. Hillary was. She was having a rough go of it personally; she and Bill were in counseling, and she wasn't ready to forgive him and wasn't sure about the future of the marriage. But she was sure that what he'd done was not a high crime or misdemeanor, and so she poured herself into helping elect more people who would agree. In *Living History*, she records hitting at least eight states. Her efforts on behalf of Charles Schumer, a member of the House from Brooklyn running for the U.S. Senate against the powerful incumbent (and Clinton antagonist) Alfonse D'Amato, were particularly noted, since they happened in the country's media capital. She visited New York four times on Schumer's behalf, and he won going away. New York's Democratic pols took note: she's gotten pretty good at this, and New Yorkers seem to like her.

In the end, the experts were about as wrong as they've ever been about an election. The Democrats actually gained five seats in the House. In the Senate, the balance of power remained unchanged. Democratic voters, it turned out, were not demoralized—they were furious, and they proved it by voting in much larger than antici-pated numbers. Black turnout was especially high for a midterm election. This was a fascinating development. Clinton's track rec-ord on racial questions had been mixed. On the one hand, he'd preserved affirmative action, largely defended civil rights, and appointed many African Americans to high positions. On the other hand, there was the Sister Souljah attack, his signing of the harsh welfare bill, and his defenestration of Lani Guinier.

The Lewinsky saga brought many black voters firmly into Clinton's corner, as well as a good percentage of the white liberal-left for whom Clinton had been too corporatist and centrist: if the Republicans hate Clinton *this* much, went the reasoning, there just may be something compelling about him that we haven't fully appreciated. In the case of African Americans, there was some-thing, too, in Clinton's biography. He was not the kind of white per-son who was remote from their experience, who'd grown up wealthy and gone to prep schools and Harvard; he was the kind of white person they knew in their daily lives. This is part of what Toni Morrison was getting at when, in early October, as the House was marching ahead with impeachment, she called Clinton "our first black president," a phrase that was immediately celebrated and derided. She argued that African American men in particular could well relate to the moralistic posturing over the president's sexuality.

Years ago, in the middle of the Whitewater investigation, one heard the first murmurs: white skin notwithstanding, this is our first black president. Blacker than any actual black person who could ever be elected in our children's lifetime.

After all, Clinton displays almost every trope of black-
ness: single-parent household, born poor, working-class,
saxophone-playing, McDonald's-and-junk-food-loving boy
from Arkansas. And when virtually all the African American
Clinton appointees began, one by one, to disappear, when
the President's body, his privacy, his unpoliced sexuality
became the focus of the persecution, when he was metaphorically seized and body-searched, who could gainsay these
black men who knew whereof they spoke?

The right had spent years stoking the culture war and placing
questions of morality at the white-hot center of American politics—
religion, abortion, gay rights, "family values," evolution, and so many
other issues had been crucial to their success and to Gingrich's
rise in particular. An infidelity committed by a man they already
regarded as a 1960s moral reprobate was something they were
bound to pursue to the bitter end. Even if Gingrich and other congressional leaders of the effort, such as Tom DeLay of Texas, the
House majority whip, were just being cynical and opportunistic
themselves, the constituents whom they'd spent a decade whipping
into moral frenzies demanded that they attempt Clinton's removal.
    But now, in the fall of 1998—the release of the prurient Starr
report, the impeachment push, the news stories that began to drib-
ble out about the elves and the Jones legal team, suggesting that
Hillary may have had a point about that conspiracy—brought
together the other side in the culture war. That side had been divided
over Clinton, at times bitterly so. But Starr and Gingrich united it,
and they even accomplished the trick of putting Team Left in a position it didn't typically find itself: on the side of the majority.

• • •

Republicans in the House had been unhappy with Newt Gingrich's
leadership for some time. His mishandling of the federal government shutdown was a big reason, as were Gingrich's own ethics
issues—his misuse of a political action committee had resulted

in the House voting overwhelmingly in January 1997 to repri-
mand him, the first time the House had ever done that to a sitting
Speaker. That summer, some Republicans attempted a coup against
him, but they couldn't marshal enough votes to oust him. And
now came this electoral disaster. Three days after it, Gingrich
shocked Washington by announcing his resignation.

The new Speaker, it soon emerged, would be Bob Livingston,
a conservative Republican from Louisiana. Some observers wondered whether the switch would lead to the party letting up on
the impeachment gas pedal, but Livingston had always been pro-
impeachment, and in any event it was really DeLay whose foot
was on the accelerator. A new Speaker is typically not elected until
the January following an election year, when the new House is first
called to order. But Livingston had the votes and was in essence
the Speaker-elect by the week after Election Day.

But something was going on in Beverly Hills that would give this
story yet one more incredible twist. Larry Flynt, the publisher of
Hustler, the pornography magazine, had a history of running often
tasteless editorial content attacking society's sexual moralists. Flynt
was so outraged by what he saw as Republican sexual hypocrisy
that he took out newspaper ads offering $1 million to anyone who
could bring him credible information about any Republican members of Congress having extramarital relations. There had long been
rumors about Gingrich himself, and indeed it later emerged that
during the entire time that Gingrich was pressing for impeachment
and thundering away about Clinton's morals, he was married to his
second wife but was having an affair with the woman who eventually became wife number three. So surely there was material
aplenty out there.

On December 11 and 12, 1998, the House Judiciary Committee voted out four articles of impeachment. They read, in order:

- That the president "provided perjurious, false, and misleading
  testimony to the grand jury regarding the Paula Jones case and
  his relationship with Monica Lewinsky."

- That he "provided perjurious, false, and misleading testimony in the Jones case in his answers to written questions and in his deposition."
- That he "obstructed justice in an effort to delay, impede, cover up, and conceal the existence of evidence related to the Jones case."
- That he "misused and abused his office by making perjurious, false, and misleading statements to Congress."

All were passed strictly along party lines, 21 to 16, except the second one, on which Clinton actually got one Republican vote, from Lindsey Graham of South Carolina, who said that the confusing definition of sexual relations in the Jones case inclined him to give the president the benefit of the doubt on this one. Now the articles would move to the full House, where everyone anticipated passage largely along party lines.

The world turned. On December 14, Clinton was in Gaza to watch in person as the Palestinians voted to end their formal call for the destruction of Israel, after landing at the new airport he'd helped create. On December 15, Iraq repeated its insistence that it would not allow reentry for the international weapons inspectors it had expelled from the country two months prior. The ominous headline on the front page of the *New York Times* read "Iraq Is Accused of New Rebuffs to UN Team; U.S. Repeats Warnings of Striking Baghdad." On a normal news day, that surely would have been the lead story, but on this day, it sat on the far-left column, straining for attention against the four-column, all-caps "WHITE HOUSE GRASPS AT OPTIONS AS WAVERERS MOVE TO IMPEACH." No one was thinking about Iraq.

And that very night the United States bombed Iraq.

Iraq's Baathist regime, which seized power in 1968, had not been something Americans needed to worry much about. In the 1970s, Baghdad tilted toward the Soviet Union; but after the Iranian Revolution of 1979, the United States slowly started buddying up to Iraq and its new leader, Saddam Hussein. When Iraq invaded Iran in 1980, the United States provided military and financial assistance to Iraq. But then everything changed after Iraq stormed into Kuwait in 1990, and President George H. W. Bush coordinated the Persian Gulf War to expel the invader. Neoconservatives inside and outside the administration wanted Bush to send the troops on to Baghdad and remove Hussein, but Bush resisted. Ousting Hussein remained very much on neocons' minds, but the project was delayed (only until 2003, as we would learn) when the country elected a Democrat in 1992.

Clinton had taken a reasonably hard line against Iraq. The official policy was "dual containment" of Iraq and Iran, but Hussein's string of small provocations drew some aggressive American responses—occasional quick bombing strikes and economic sanctions that many international observers considered so severe as to be inhumane. All this time, under the terms of Iraq's surrender in the Gulf War, and because Hussein had used poison gas on his own subjects (the Kurds in the north), the regime was subject to regular weapons inspections. In August, Hussein curtailed the inspectors' activities, before cutting them off altogether in October. Then, on December 15, 1998, the United Nations released a report detailing the many ways in which Iraq had blocked inspectors from doing their work; hence, the bombing.

Was it another *Wag the Dog* scenario? Many Republicans and talking heads thought so. Clinton insisted it was not. "If we had delayed for even a matter of days from [the UN] report, we would have given Saddam more time to disperse his forces and protect his weapons," Clinton told the nation from the Oval Office. He noted also that Ramadan started that weekend, and that bombing during the holy month "would be profoundly offensive to the Muslim world and, therefore, would damage our relations with Arab countries and the progress we have made in the Middle East." The raids continued for four days. (In fact, the bombing of Iraq never really stopped during Clinton's presidency, to enforce a Western-imposed no-fly zone.)

The House readied for its votes, which were set for Saturday,

December 19. But before that, one more bolt of lightning would strike. On Thursday, rumors began circulating about the Speaker-elect. By that night, Livingston had made a shocking admission, seemingly out of nowhere: yes, he admitted, he had had adulterous affairs. The next day, Friday, the nation saw why he'd made his pre-emptive admission. Larry Flynt announced that he had the goods: proof, he said, that Livingston had had extramarital affairs with four women.

Livingston took to the floor of the House on Saturday. He called on Clinton to resign. Democrats shouted: "No! You resign!" And very soon in that same speech Livingston did. The hunting of the president had not taken Clinton down, but it did ensnare two Republican Speakers, the second of whom never even officially held the job. Only two of the four articles of impeachment passed—the first, about misleading testimony to the Paula Jones grand jury, and the third, which charged obstruction of justice. But two were enough. It was on to the Senate for trial, for only the second time in American history. Clinton appeared on the South Lawn of the White House—arm in arm with Hillary, who now saw their job as defending the Constitution—and said he planned to stay on the job "until the last hour" and "to go on from here to rise above the ran-cor, to overcome the pain and division, to be a repairer of the breach."

10

Ducking Lightning Bolts
Till the End

At 10:05 a.m. on Thursday, January 7, 1999, the House managers—
the thirteen Republican members of the House who would present the evidence against Clinton in his impeachment trial, acting
in essence as the prosecution team—filed into the chamber of the
United States Senate. They were escorted to the well, whereupon
the Senate's sergeant at arms, James Ziglar, announced: "Hear ye!
Hear ye! Hear ye! All persons are commanded to keep silent, on
pain of imprisonment, while the House of Representatives is
exhibiting to the Senate of the United States articles of impeachment against William Jefferson Clinton, President of the United
States."

There was much custom and pomp. Everyone spoke solemnly.
Chief justice William H. Rehnquist, assigned by the Constitution
to act as presiding judge, sat up above the litigants in a robe embroidered with four gold stripes on each arm, an adornment that he
said was inspired by a costume he'd seen in a local production of
Gilbert and Sullivan's *Iolanthe*. Senators and the House managers
debated whether witnesses would be called, and how many, and
whether they would testify in person or on videotape. Monica
Lewinsky, mobbed by the media on her return to Washington, was
deposed on videotape. The media treated it all portentously.

But the truth was that there was no drama to the proceedings at all. Moment to moment, they were mostly, in fact, boring. In real life, trials are long and technical and don't make for good television. But the main thing was this: under the Constitution, two-thirds of senators must vote to convict for a president to be removed from office. Though the Republicans controlled the new Senate 55 to 45, there was no way that twelve Democrats were going to desert Clinton, and everyone knew it. Yet the House Republicans pressed on with their "onerous, miserable, rotten" duty.

There was one moment of drama that month, and it happened not in the Senate chamber but in the House: Clinton's State of the Union address, delivered that year on January 19, in the midst of the trial. Tensions were high in the chamber as the president spoke; top Republicans Tom DeLay and Dick Armey sat next to each other in prominent seats, pointedly never applauding once, not even when Clinton was introduced. Clinton, as he had done the previous year, strolled through it all as if nothing in the world were out of the ordinary. Finally, on February 12, 1999, the senators voted. The first count, for perjury, was defeated 45 in favor, 55 against. The second count, for obstruction, ended in a 50–50 tie. Clinton strolled into the Rose Garden after the vote and delivered a contrite, four-sentence statement, and nearly thirteen months after the world first heard the name *Monica Lewinsky* it was over.

Something arguably much more interesting happened inside the White House on February 12. At around the same time the Senate was casting its votes, Hillary Clinton called in Harold Ickes to ask him questions about New York. Three days after Chuck Schumer beat Alfonse D'Amato with Hillary's help in that 1998 Senate race, New York's respected senior senator, Daniel Patrick Moynihan, announced his retirement from the U.S. Senate. New York was at that point bereft of any first-tier Democrats who seemed an obvious choice to succeed the man who to many epitomized what a senator ought to be. The Republicans, meanwhile, had Governor George Pataki and Mayor Rudy Giuliani, both formidable politicians. It began to dawn on New York Democrats that they should recruit Hillary to run for Moynihan's seat. She summoned Ickes, who had come of age in the cauldron of New York politics, to pepper him with questions. He had one for her: "Why in God's name would you want to do this?" But as she kept pressing, it became clear to him that "she was going to have to be talked out of it."

. . .

On Monday, March 29, 1999, a milestone was hit as the Dow Jones Industrial Average closed above 10,000 for the first time ever. On the day Clinton took office, the Dow had stood at 3,241. It was yet another marker, along with the 22 million jobs that were ultimately created and the staggering 11 percent growth in median household income—greater than under any other president since those data were first gathered in 1967—of how the economy had roared under Clinton. Clearly, not all of it was his doing; some of it was the Federal Reserve's doing, as is always the case, and, of course, the spread of the Internet and the huge tech boom helped. It also helped, in terms of how Clinton came to be remembered, that he got out just in time—the so-called dot-com bubble started to pop in the spring of 2000, but the country didn't face recession until Clinton left office.

His job-approval numbers had slipped a hair from the previous summer's highs north of 70 percent, but he was still in the low 60s; he'd survived impeachment; the political class was beginning to turn its attention to the next presidential election; he was in a position to coast to the end. What would he do with the remaining seven hundred or so days in office? He would turn mostly to foreign policy, to two matters that had consumed him from his earliest days. He was determined not to leave office without brokering a Middle East peace deal. But before he could get to that in earnest, he would need to confront Slobodan Milosevic one final time.

In the months since Richard Holbrooke had read the riot act to Milosevic in July 1998, fighting in Kosovo had continued. Holbrooke helped arrange a cease-fire in October. Sporadic battles flared up again in December, and then in January 1999 came the Račak Massacre, in which Serbian forces killed forty-five Kosovar Albanians in retaliation for a KLA attack on four Serb policemen. Milosevic expelled the American ambassador. Talks on Kosovar autonomy were held in Rambouillet, France, in a grand château where NATO and Russian negotiators couldn't even put the Serbs and the Kosovars in the same room, such was the level of antagonism. The talks stalled and were extended and moved to Paris; on March 19, they broke down, as the Serbs refused to agree to any form of autonomy and walked away. Some critics charged that NATO had drafted an agreement the Serbs couldn't possibly sign by demanding free movement for NATO forces throughout not just Kosovo but Serbia itself; but British foreign secretary Robin Cook told the BBC a year later that "if that particular technical annex was something that bothered them, we would have been very happy to have considered constructive amendments from them. They never even raised it."

Four days later, the bombs—NATO bombs, officially, not American ones—began falling on Serbia. This campaign would last not just a day, as the bin Laden strike had, or a few days, as was the case with the bombing of Iraq. It carried on for eleven weeks. This time, there was no *Wag the Dog* catcalling. Milosevic had bedeviled Clinton since nearly the day he took office, and Europe had certainly had enough of the man who had arguably wreaked more havoc on the continent than anyone since Hitler.

It didn't all go without a hitch, though. On May 7, 1999, bombs struck the Chinese embassy in Belgrade, killing three Chinese citizens. The bombs had not gone astray: they'd hit their intended target, but, incredibly, the maps NATO was using (provided by the CIA) had identified the building as a Serbian government building that was used for military purposes. The Chinese were enraged and accused the Americans of an intentional attack. For a full week, Jiang Zemin wouldn't even take the calls of the president of the United States. When they did finally speak, Clinton recalled,

I apologized again and told him I was sure he didn't believe I would knowingly attack his embassy. Jiang replied that he knew I wouldn't do that, but said he did believe that there were people in the Pentagon or the CIA who didn't favor my outreach to China and could have rigged the maps intentionally to cause a rift between us.

In time, the matter was smoothed out. The bombing was halted on June 10. Around five hundred Serbian and Kosovar civilians were killed; the United States lost just two soldiers. It took a while to bring Milosevic down, but the next fall he was defeated in an election and shortly hauled off to The Hague to face a war crimes tribunal.

· · ·

The closing months of a presidential administration are a time when issues that hadn't received much prominence before can be elevated. Such was the case with Bill Clinton and the environment. He had not been much of an environmentalist as governor of Arkansas, operating in a poor and rural state where public sentiment would always support jobs and growth over environmental concerns. He came into office promising to reduce carbon emissions and take other measures to fight the effects of climate change, which science had recognized since the late 1980s as a threat partially caused by human activity.

Clinton's Republican predecessor George H. W. Bush had accepted the science and instructed the Environmental Protection Agency to pursue solutions; Clinton did the same, appointing solid environmentalists to key positions. But when the Gingrich Congress came in, the Republicans swerved hard to the right on these issues; the "job-destroying" EPA occupied a place of prominence on the new right's enemies list. Many of Clinton's actions on behalf of the environment took the form of staving off attempts by Republicans to weaken regulations or gut the Endangered Species Act. There

were times, however, when Clinton directly angered environmentalists, as when he signed an appropriations bill in 1995 that allowed
for so-called salvage logging of trees killed either by insects or in a
wildfire in a way that permitted logging companies to step around
the normal rules and processes. The Republicans had pushed for this
measure in the wake of the previous year's rampant wildfires in
the West. Bruce Babbitt, Clinton's secretary of the interior, toed
the line publicly but privately was said to believe the White House
"gave away the store" when it agreed to the salvage rider. Both
Clinton and Vice President Gore, the administration's greenie-in-
residence, later admitted the rider was a mistake.

Now, though, Clinton set off on a veritable conservation spree.
In his last two years in office he placed vast parcels of land under
federal protection. In January 2000, it was a million acres around
the Grand Canyon and islands off the California coast; in May, an
initiative to protect coasts and coral reefs; and, just two weeks
before leaving office, sixty million acres of national forest. Clinton
relied on the 1906 Antiquities Act as his authority for much of
this activity, and in the end he was said to have "set aside more
acreage under the Act than Theodore Roosevelt," widely considered
America's greatest environmentalist president.

But the core focus of Clinton's final year in office was the Middle
East. President Carter had secured peace between Israel and Egypt
in 1978. In 1994, Clinton had helped orchestrate a historic peace
treaty between Israel and Jordan, which had controlled the West
Bank prior to the 1967 war. But peace between the Israelis and the
Palestinians themselves, with so many vexing issues that struck so
deep inside both people's identities and histories and that seemed
so hopelessly insoluble, had eluded every president who'd tried.

The new Israeli prime minister, Ehud Barak, was a highly decorated army officer who had once dressed as a woman in an under-
cover operation in Beirut to kill Palestinians who were deemed to
have had Israeli blood on their hands. Now he clearly wanted to go
down in history as the man who ended the tensions. He wanted
peace not just with the Palestinians but also with Lebanon, which

had been officially at war with Israel since the latter's formation in 1948, and with Syria, from which Israel had taken the Golan Heights in 1967. In 1999, Barak began pushing Clinton to start the process with Syria. And so in January 2000, Clinton gathered the two parties together in Shepherdstown, West Virginia, a hamlet up in the hills a little more than an hour's drive northwest of Washington. Barak came ready to deal, and the Syrians, under President Hafez al-Assad, responded in kind. But when the moment of truth came, Barak blinked, perhaps fearful of a backlash at home. The parties, and the president, walked away empty-handed. A few months later, when Clinton tried to reignite the talks, Assad was in failing health and no longer interested. A major opportunity was missed to show the region, and the world, that these historic enemies could make peace.

Clinton pressed on. On July 11, 2000, at Camp David, he opened direct talks between the Israelis and the Palestinians. Again, Barak had pushed for the summit; Arafat had been more ambivalent. A few days into the meeting, Israel made significant moves on the status of Jerusalem and on the amount of occupied territory it would yield to a new Palestinian state. Arafat didn't budge for a while, but he finally produced a letter that "seemed to say," as Clinton put it in *My Life*, "that if he was satisfied with the Jerusalem question, I could make the final call on how much land the Israelis kept for settlements and what constituted a fair land swap."

On the seventh day, Barak choked on a peanut and stopped breathing for nearly forty seconds before getting a Heimlich from someone and gathering himself. That night, or, in fact, in the wee hours of the next morning, he gave Clinton permission to see if he could work out a deal with Arafat on Jerusalem and the settlements. The next day, Clinton presented Arafat with a plan that included many Israeli concessions but not full Palestinian sovereignty over the Temple Mount—or "Haram al-Sharif" to the Muslims—home to the Dome of the Rock and the Al-Aqsa Mosque but also the holiest site in Judaism. Arafat said no.

Clinton then flew to Okinawa for a G-8 summit for four days.

He returned and pushed both sides hard—more three a.m. negotiations. The two sides were closer than they'd ever been. There was little substantive disagreement anymore, but both parties, Arafat especially, were hung up over the word *sovereignty*. When it finally became clear to Clinton that there was no budging them on this point, he suspended the talks. But he now said he had "a better idea of each side's bottom line."

· · ·

It was the heat of the political season. Vice President Al Gore would be running against Governor George W. Bush of Texas, son of the former president. With the nation at peace and the economy still humming along nicely, it shouldn't have been a difficult election for Gore. But the incumbent party always has a hard time winning a third term, and Gore tied himself in knots trying to embrace Clinton's policy legacy while simultaneously distancing himself from Clinton's personal failings. Tensions between the two men were said to be high, but it didn't prevent the president from giving a valedictory speech to the Democratic convention in Los Angeles that made a better case for Gore than Gore could make for himself. Gore spent most of the year just trailing Bush in the polls.

It had been a rocky year on the trail for Hillary, too. At first she had been running against Mayor Giuliani, whose record of stunning success in crime fighting was offset by a habit of going out of his way to alienate groups that didn't vote for him, especially African Americans. But in the late spring, Giuliani got caught up in his own sex scandal, as an extramarital affair that he'd made surprisingly little effort to hide was finally exposed. Then he was diagnosed with prostate cancer. He quit the race, replaced by Congressman Rick Lazio, who upon entry seemed to be a formidable candidate against Clinton—being Italian and from Long Island and a moderate-to-conservative Republican were three good things to be in those days when seeking statewide office in New York. And Clinton, unlike her husband, was not a natural on the campaign trail.

In the fall of an election year when the incumbent isn't running, no one in the political world pays much attention to the president, unless something newsworthy happens. And on October 12, 2000, something did. The navy guided-missile destroyer the USS *Cole* was harbored in the port of Aden, Yemen, for a routine refueling stop when a small fiberglass boat carrying explosives and two suicide bombers rammed the vessel's port side. The bomb made a fifty-foot gash in the ship; seventeen sailors were killed and thirty-nine injured. Al-Qaeda had struck again. Or so it was presumed—but not, at the time, verified. Clinton wanted to strike at bin Laden one more time, but without a clear finding of al-Qaeda's responsibility his hands were tied. (Bin Laden would claim responsibility in a March 2001 video.)

Surprisingly, the bombing didn't reverberate loudly in the presidential contest. But in the New York Senate race, the state Republican Party was paying for robocalls to voters saying that Hillary Clinton had accepted money from an Arab organization that "openly brags about its support for a Mideast terrorism group, the same kind of terrorism that killed our sailors on the USS *Cole*." Whether New Yorkers had or had not come to love Hillary, the idea that the First Lady of the United States consorted with *Cole* bombing–types was a bit much. Once again, the right, in its Clinton hatred, had gone too far and had presumed that less ideologically motivated voters shared all their negative presumptions about the Clintons. She handled her debates and the pressure of the campaign's final days well, and by the time election night rolled around, she'd racked up an eight-point win over Lazio and would become a U.S. senator for a state where she had never lived.

The mood was festive in her Manhattan hotel victory-party ballroom—until the large television screens flashed the news that the networks were putting Florida, previously called for Gore, back into the too-close-to-call camp. The drama and trauma that gripped the nation for the next month was not, strictly speaking, for the incumbent president to comment on. It was his duty to ensure an orderly transfer of power, and he would do so. When the Supreme Court handed down its decision in *Bush v. Gore*, giving the presidency to George W. Bush, Clinton released a statement noting that the "closely divided" court had spoken, praising both candidates, and calling for national unity. Later, in *My Life*, he put it far more bluntly: "It was an appalling decision. A narrow conservative majority that had made a virtual fetish of states' rights had now stripped Florida of a clear state function: the right to recount the votes the way it always had."

The fact that the next president was going to be Bush, who would surely tilt much more in Israel's direction, helped give Clinton even more impetus to encourage the Palestinians to come back to the table for one last push for peace. Israeli and Palestinian teams traveled to Washington, where they began meetings in mid-December at Bolling Air Force Base. On December 23, Clinton brought the negotiators to the White House. He sat them down in the Cabinet Room and slowly read to them his "parameters" for final negotiation toward striking a deal—how much of the West Bank the Palestinians would get, the size of the land swap that Israel would get, the status of Jerusalem, refugees, security agreements—everything. There were minor details to be agreed to, but these broad parameters, the president said, were nonnegotiable.

They broke for Christmas. On December 27, a huge breakthrough: Barak's cabinet accepted the terms—an Israeli government was ready to end the occupation and say yes to a Palestinian state. Arafat equivocated. Clinton called other Arab leaders, including Egypt's president Hosni Mubarak, urging them to tell Arafat to take the deal. On January 2, 2001, he brought Arafat to the White House. Arafat asked questions. But Clinton could tell from Arafat's body language that he didn't have the guts to take the step to become a peacemaker, to endure the rage that would surely have been directed at him from his radical flank. He never said no outright, but he never said yes. Clinton and others tried to lay out to him the implications of walking away—Bush was coming in, the Israeli right (led now by Ariel Sharon) would surely win the next election in the wake of a collapse, and peace would become an impossibility. But he froze. Shortly before Clinton left office, Arafat called him to thank him for his efforts and tell him he was a great man. "I am not a great man," the president replied. "I am a failure, and you have made me one."

. . .

The previous president to serve two full terms, Ronald Reagan, floated out of the White House on vast clouds of goodwill. Clinton careened out of the place ducking lightning bolts. True to form, he did one or two things that gave his critics some material, and—true to form—those critics went overboard in exaggerating and even fabricating allegations of misconduct, which the media, also true to form, gobbled up voraciously.

On his last day in office, Clinton announced the traditional set of presidential pardons. Recipients included the faithful and courageous Susan McDougal, whom Ken Starr had kept in prison and even solitary confinement because she wouldn't say what he wanted her to say about Clinton; Dan Rostenkowski, the longtime chairman of the House Ways and Means Committee laid low in a banking scandal; two female members of the radical Weather Underground; Patty Hearst, the heiress who'd joined another radical group in the 1970s; and the president's own brother, Roger, pardoned on drug-related charges even though he had already served his term.

These provoked the usual amounts of sputtering. But then there was Marc Rich, who owed $48 million in back taxes and had fled justice, living in Switzerland, and whose estranged wife, Denise, was a big Clinton donor. The howls of indignation were ferocious. For a couple of hours on the closing moments of Clinton's 2,922nd day in office, it was almost like the Lewinsky scandal again, as cable talking heads literally screamed in disbelief that Clinton could do such a thing. Clinton maintained that he was following the recommendation of his Justice Department—specifically, Eric Holder—and that Rich would still be subject to civil legal action. It was also the case that Ehud Barak had intervened with Clinton three times on Rich's behalf. (Rich had spent some time in Israel and engaged in much philanthropy there.) But from the point of view of appearances, it was a hard decision to defend.

In the succeeding days, another story went viral—that the Clintons had "stolen" furniture that properly belonged not to them but to the White House and had hauled it up to their new home in New York. Again, they were accused of all manner of thievery; again, a lot of what was said simply wasn't true. They had received nearly fifteen thousand gifts in eight years. The system to log them was a mess; it turned out that they had taken a handful of items that the donors had intended for the White House permanent collection, and the Clintons returned them (and ultimately had three of those gifts returned back to them after it was determined that they were right to have taken them).

Then there was the matter of Hillary's alleged "gift registry" at Borsheims, a high-end Nebraska retailer. The idea here was that as an incoming senator, Hillary would be subject to strict gift rules, so she supposedly contacted all her friends and asked them to buy her fancy things before she was sworn in so she could skirt the ethics rules. It fit perfectly into the narrative of Hillary as that entitled rhymes-with-witch that the media had pushed since 1992. She did receive some gifts from friends via Borsheims, sixteen soup bowls and a tureen, but no hard evidence was ever produced that she'd "registered like a bride," as she was often accused of having done.

And, finally, there was the scandal of the missing Ws. Here, it was alleged that Clinton aides had left the West Wing in a tatty state for the incoming Bush aides: file cabinets glued shut, presidential seals steamed off doors, wires cut. And, most shockingly of all, Ws yanked off computer keyboards, mocking the new president's middle initial and sobriquet. The message of this story? "The trailer-trash Clintons and their staff had enjoyed one last bacchanal at taxpayer expense," as *Salon*'s Eric Boehlert put it. The only problem was that the entire story was apparently a fabrication. Four months later, a Government Accounting Office report found that there was "no damage to the offices of the White House's East or West Wings or [Executive Office Building]," and that Bush's own representatives had reported "there is no record of damage that may have been deliberately caused by the employees of the Clinton administration."

It was a crazy ending, but it was inevitable that Bill Clinton would go out the way he came in, embattled and taking enormous amounts of incoming fire. And he did it with his usual astonishing ability to compartmentalize and glide through it. On his final day in office, at the exact same moment that the news channels were pulverizing him over the Marc Rich pardon, Clinton went to Andrews Air Force Base to take his last flight on Air Force One, up to his new home in Westchester County, New York; in the hangar, he gave one last speech to his supporters. The crowd held aloft placards saying "Thank You" and "Please Don't Go"; the president smiled contentedly as he repeated three times: "We did a lot of good." The last public sentence he uttered that day, aside from "Thank you" and "God bless you," was: "You gave me the ride of my life, and I tried to give as good as I got." It was an absolutely fitting pugilistic image with which to conclude a turbulent eight years. The attacks never stopped but, as he had with that ram those many years before, he absorbed them all and survived.

Epilogue

Sunday, January 21, 2001, was the first morning in eighteen years—ten as governor, eight as president—that Bill Clinton woke up without someone to make his breakfast. A small entourage of friends was staying with him and Hillary at the Clintons' chosen new home in Chappaqua, New York, and Bill suggested that the group venture out to the village's small downtown for coffee and breakfast. As Joe Conason tells the story in *Man of the World*, his book on Clinton's post-presidency, the customers at Lang's Little Shop and Delicatessen greeted him with chants of "Eight more years!" But another, less enthusiastic assemblage was gathered out on the sidewalk—a dozen or so reporters, screaming questions about the Marc Rich pardon.

The Rich story didn't die, really, until late that summer. Official Washington was enraged at the pardon, and somehow Clinton hadn't grasped how negatively it would be seen. Denise Rich, the fugitive's ex-wife, had donated more than $500,000 to the Democratic Party, and the pardon was universally seen as payback to her. House Republicans again held hearings and issued subpoenas. For a while, there loomed the possibility of a federal criminal investigation. At the same time, cable outrage continued over the White House gifts matter and the supposed purloined keyboard *W*s. Clinton himself stayed barricaded in his new home, fixated on the cable news, fuming. Friends implored him to quit watching. Conason writes: "He would promise to stop, and then get on the phone with friends and ask whether they had seen the latest cable TV slurs against him."

It was bad. And, incredibly, it got worse. Former presidents need office space, for which the taxpayers foot the bill. For his, Clinton initially chose one of the newest and most expensive pieces of commercial real estate in all of midtown Manhattan—the top floor of a fifty-six-story skyscraper, the Carnegie Hall Tower, which had been recently erected on West 57th Street, adjacent to the legendary Carnegie Hall. The annual rent would run north of $600,000, which was more than the government was spending on all the other living ex-presidents *combined*. It was an unimaginably perception-blind choice. Again, Congress intervened, advising that an appropriate amount would be nearer $200,000. After some absolutely brutal tabloid headlines and cable news segments, the aide who had originally identified the Carnegie space, Karen Tramontano, passed along to Clinton a suggestion she'd received from Congressman Charlie Rangel—that Clinton consider setting up his office in the Adam Clayton Powell State Office Building on West 125th Street in Harlem, which would cost a fraction of the Carnegie rent. Clinton resisted at first—he saw it as backing down to the mob, Conason writes—but as he considered the new round of merciless coverage and thought through the matter, he came to see the public-relations benefit of relocating to a neighborhood where his approval rating was surely around 90 percent, for which he could perform many a good deed—and where the residents didn't care very much about Marc Rich.

So proceeded the turbulent launch of the most controversial ex-presidency in recent or maybe all of American history. The gravity of these early missteps was intensified by the financial pressure both Clintons were feeling, having left the White House with $11 million in legal bills. Hillary, as a senator, was proscribed from earning more than her Senate salary, owing to stricter new ethics guidelines, although she had made sure to sign a book deal before beginning her term, for a reported $8 million. (The Senate Ethics Committee gave its approval.) Bill stood to make plenty of money from speeches and a memoir of his own. But after the successive waves of scorching press coverage, many groups that had invited him to speak were canceling left and right. The Clinton Presidential Library in Little Rock still needed to raise tens of millions of dollars to get off the ground—and donors to that enterprise were now getting calls from FBI investigators, asking why exactly they had donated and if they were seeking a favor in return. Clinton was damaged goods, more so than he had ever been as president, when he had a vast support network of staff and activists willing to go to the mat for him, and when he was, after all, the leader of the free world.

Now, without millions of Americans rising to his defense, and with the country having moved on, he sat at home in Chappaqua, alone more often than he preferred, figuring out this new TiVo device his friend Steven Spielberg had given him as a gift, catching up on the television shows of the 1990s that he'd been too busy to watch.

• • •

As noted in chapter 1, the assessments of Bill Clinton's legacy as president by historians and political scientists have generally been kind—and increasingly so over the years. No doubt the prosperous Clinton economy has had a lot to do with that, especially given what has happened in the years since (wage stagnation, growing inequality, the 2008 financial crisis, and more). His conduct of foreign policy, too, came to look quite good in retrospect. Also embroidered within those assessments, perhaps, was a collective view that whatever his flaws, he faced an opposition more relentless than any president before him had been forced to do battle with, and that the impeachment was partisan and unjustified by the facts.

But Clinton's legacy cannot be limited to those eight years, for two main reasons. First, he chose an unusually public path after leaving the White House, in the way he built and ran his foundation, and in earning such enormous sums of money from the speeches he delivered to various groups, businesses, and organizations. In contrast, his successor, George W. Bush, rarely gave speeches, never commented on public affairs, and sat at home painting his canvases. But Clinton decided to make himself a very public figure, which naturally invited more scrutiny from a press corps always on the lookout for a Clinton scandal story to write. And second, of course, his wife remained active in politics and was the Democratic Party's nominee for president in 2016.

The William J. Clinton Foundation (later renamed the Bill, Hillary, and Chelsea Clinton Foundation) was originally perceived in modest terms. It was established in 1997 to raise funds for Clinton's presidential library, but as Clinton settled into his new Harlem office, events began to suggest to him that the foundation could operate on a much grander scale. A horrible earthquake in the Gujarat province of India in late January 2001 afforded him his first post-presidential opportunity to do urgent humanitarian work. Residents and business people in Harlem, upon learning that he and his staff would be headquartered in their famous but impoverished neighborhood, flooded him with requests for philanthropic assistance. And, of course, he knew people. All over the world. Heads of state, potentates, and really, really, really rich people. And if he had one great, innate skill in life, going back to those high school days when he couldn't get good citizenship marks because he wouldn't stop talking, it was schmoozing people.

Thus did the foundation became an enormous, sprawling venture. In early 2002 Clinton decided, with the help of Ira Magaziner, who'd worked with the Clintons on health care reform, that the main focus would be fighting the spread of AIDS in Africa. This, too, grew from an early post-presidential experience, an April 2001 AIDS conference that Clinton attended in Abuja, Nigeria. There was no consensus in 2002 that the incidence of AIDS in the less-developed world even could be arrested; initially, most public health experts in the West whose cooperation Clinton sought turned him down cold, notes Conason. But Clinton didn't accept this bleak reality and felt that it could be changed if pharmaceutical companies could be persuaded to provide anti-AIDS drugs at lower prices,

and if Western governments would finance health care infrastructure in developing nations.

And so, with Magaziner attending to much of the detail, the
foundation announced a deal in October 2003 under which generic
drug manufacturers agreed to slash the price of antiretroviral
medicine while also laying out plans for massive investments in
health care facilities in developing nations. It was a groundbreak-
ing agreement whose terms expanded over the years, and experts
attest that it surely saved millions of lives. The foundation's work
would later extend into a broad range of areas: fighting childhood
obesity in the United States, helping farmers in the developing
world, launching initiatives designed to combat the effects of global
warming, and more.

For a time, the foundation got positive press. A lot of it. The Clinton HIV-AIDS Initiative benefited Clinton greatly in reputational
terms at first, helping him crawl out of the Marc Rich–Carnegie
Tower ditch that he'd been in since early 2001. He took more hits
from the right after September 11, when the right-wing media decided to blame him for the attacks on New York and Washington,
partly because he hadn't killed or captured bin Laden during his
time in office, but mostly as a way to deflect any blame that might
be placed on President Bush. But those attacks didn't really take
hold among the general populace. Through the mid-2000s, with
Hillary serving diligently in the Senate, and Bill publishing his
autobiography *My Life*, for which he was paid a reported $15
million—and with the first stories of his heart problems rendering
him a more sympathetic figure (he would eventually require qua-
druple bypass surgery)—he was doing all right in terms of his public
image.

But the worm began to turn in January 2008, when the *New York
Times* published a long story suggesting that Clinton had pulled
strings to help a wealthy foundation donor secure a mining deal
in Kazakhstan. It was revealed over time that some of the story's
particulars were aggressively challenged by other journalists. But
the damage was done. The foundation's reputation began to corrode

inside political circles; critics now cast what was once seen as a benign and noble philanthropic endeavor as an enterprise that existed chiefly for the purpose of allowing Bill Clinton to jet around the world in the private planes of multimillionaires. Around this same time, the former president was acquitting himself poorly in his wife's first presidential run, when he launched attacks on Senator Barack Obama that seemed out of character for him—jumping on Obama's lack of experience and at one point comparing his candidacy to Jesse Jackson's, which some African American Democratic leaders said relegated Obama to being a protest candidate. Then, after Obama's victory in the 2008 general election, Hillary became secretary of state, which meant that Bill was jetting around the globe raising money from foreign governments, sometimes from dictators, while she was trying to conduct diplomacy. By the time Hillary was gearing up for another presidential run, in 2014 and early 2015, the foundation was seen by most Washington insiders as a clear political liability.

In philanthropic journals, one could find many positive articles about the Clinton Foundation's continuing good deeds. But who read those? In the mainstream press, the foundation was just another vehicle the Clintons had found for enriching themselves, and a huge looming conflict of interest for Hillary, should she win.

The "enriching themselves" story line had legs because of the paid speeches both Clintons gave for many years for anywhere from $100,000 to as much as $500,000 a speech. The Clintons' overall net worth as of this writing is a matter of dispute but is generally pegged at something in the neighborhood of $60 million or more. Even some of their supporters questioned the zealousness of this pursuit. Certainly they were entitled to earn that $11 million to cover their legal fees, incurred through the ferocity of their political opponents. And certainly they were entitled to live on Easy Street, if that's what they wanted. But did they really need $60 million? It reeked of cashing in on the presidency. Bill

Clinton did enormous good through his foundation, but the good was tarnished by mistakes that he could so easily have avoided.

. . .

All of those errors were supposed to be wiped from the slate in November 2016, when Hillary Clinton finally completed her long march to the presidency. Her victory, which seemed assured up to the moment the polls closed on Election Day, was supposed to write the next chapter of Clintonism.

It didn't happen. Her shocking loss to Donald J. Trump was a rebuke to her first and foremost. The rebuke had many causes. Some were her fault, others were not; and certainly some people were lying to pollsters about their true feelings about the candidates— either not being willing to admit to another human being that they planned on voting for Trump or not acknowledging that they were uncomfortable voting for a woman. But it was hard to avoid the verdict, on the morning after, that a lot of Americans simply didn't trust or like her. A quarter century spent as a walking Rorschach test of America's attitudes about feminism had taken its toll.

The campaign and its result also constituted a repudiation of Bill Clinton. In the years since the economic meltdown, sentiment within portions of the rank and file of the Democratic Party, pushed in the primaries by independent voters, moved to the left on various matters, most notably trade and other issues relating to the deindustrialization of many parts of America that Trump exploited. Hillary tried to head this off and took positions at odds with her husband's stances in 1992 and 1996, on race and criminal justice, banking, regulation, and especially trade, in an effort to blunt the criticisms that came from the left in the form of Senator Bernie Sanders of Vermont, her opponent in the Democratic primaries, and his followers, and from the right in the form of the populist Donald Trump.

In fairness to Bill Clinton, he was elected by a very different America than the one that existed in 2016. On the issue of crime, for instance, as he took office in January 1993 he was looking at sky-high crime rates and a strongly held perception among white Americans that the Democratic Party was virtually on the side of the criminals. And Clinton had shown courage in these areas, for example in passing the assault weapons ban and the Violence Against Women Act. But all this was of no interest to the younger racial-justice activists of 2016. The fact that more than two-thirds of the Congressional Black Caucus had supported the 1994 crime bill—as had then-congressman Bernie Sanders—did not impress them or give them pause. They became convinced that Bill Clinton had locked up a generation of innocent black men. And so in July 2015, as Hillary's campaign was grappling with this reassessment of her husband's legacy, Bill was forced to address his role in mass incarceration, saying, "I signed a bill that made the problem worse and I want to admit it." Hillary Clinton endorsed a softening of the 1994 bill's sentencing guidelines.

She tried, within her zone of comfort, to re-tailor Clintonism to these different times, but she failed. Results are results, and the very first verdicts after the election about how the defeat would affect Bill Clinton's legacy were harsh. The first charge in this indictment of Bill Clinton invariably centered on free trade and the effects of globalization on the white working-class voters who flocked to Trump. NAFTA became the symbolic bogeyman here, and to a lesser extent the law Clinton signed in the final months of his presidency normalizing trade relations with China (to a lesser extent in terms of public debate, although most experts agree that over the years the China trade bill has had a more dramatic impact on American jobs than NAFTA). Hillary took a beating on the issue from both Sanders and Trump, such that she repudiated President Obama's signature trade pact, the Trans-Pacific Partnership, which she had helped negotiate as secretary of state.

Trump and Sanders both railed against the global elites who'd thrown the American worker into these rough seas. The Clintons were members of this elite, no doubt, and to the extent that this elite collectively failed blue-collar workers in the developed world, they deserved to be held to account. At the same time, assigning blame to something as huge and amorphous as "the global elites" is demagogic. A more nuanced view would note that American workers' incomes went up substantially during Bill Clinton's presidency and that much of the manufacturing decline in the United States has simply been a consequence of automation. Beyond that, Bill Clinton was known to be telling Hillary and her advisers that she had to speak more directly to white working-class voters on the campaign trail, advice that wasn't heeded to the extent it clearly should have been. The political result was a disaster for Democrats—not only did Trump win the presidency, but so many states that Bill Clinton had flipped to the Democratic column, states that had seemed secure for more than two decades, fell to the Republicans.

Thus did the Clinton era, and Clintonism more broadly, come to an abrupt and horrifying close. Agreeing that "the Clinton project in national governance has seemingly come to an end," Ed Kilgore, a journalist for *New York* magazine who had worked in Democratic politics and had been a devout New Democrat in the 1990s, pinpointed the specific assumption at the center of Clintonism that events had rendered inoperative:

> Central to the entire Clintonian New Democratic movement (of which I was a loyal foot soldier for a long time) was the belief that the best way to achieve progressive policy goals was by harnessing and redirecting the wealth that a less-regulated and more-innovative private sector alone could generate. That seemed to work during the late 1990s and sporadically even later. But the economic collapse at the end of the Bush administration and the struggle to head off growing inequality throughout the Obama administration has made the create-then-redistribute model for Democratic economic policy less and less satisfying, while creating a backlash among those who view any Democratic cheerleading for the private sector—especially the financial community—as a de

facto act of betrayal signaling a high probability of personal corruption.

Of course, Clinton isn't responsible for the economic decisions of his successor, decisions he regularly denounced. History always outraces politics, and events frequently change our perceptions of historical eras and presidential tenures. In time, when the Democrats have regained power, the sting of the incomprehensible 2016 defeat will soften, and the part where Bill Clinton rescued the Democratic Party from possible permanent minority status will get a new hearing. But Kilgore's assessment captured a crisis of the Democratic Party that was every bit as real as the one that led to Bill Clinton's rise to the presidency in 1992—a humbling irony of our time.

Notes

1. A YOUNG FELLOW IN A HURRY

1 "Soon he caught me and knocked my legs out": Bill Clinton, *My Life* (New York: Alfred A. Knopf, 2004), p. 22.

1 "I could take a hard hit": Ibid.

2 Clinton consistently ranked as America's most popular recent ex-president: See, for example, a June 2014 Gallup survey rating Clinton the most popular ex-president with a 64–33 favorable-to-unfavorable rating, at http://www.gallup.com/poll/171794/clinton-elder-bush-positively-rated-living-presidents.aspx.

2 he'd jumped up several notches: A February 2015 assessment by the American Political Science Association ranked Clinton the eighth best president. See, for example, "Bill Clinton Ranks High in New Historical Presidents Study," National Constitution Center, February 17, 2015, http://blog.constitutioncenter.org/2015/02/bill-clinton-ranks-high-in-new-historical-presidents-study/.

4 "everything in the house revolved around the golden son": David Maraniss, *First in His Class: A Biography of Bill Clinton* (New York: Simon & Schuster, 1996), p. 41.

4 "I loved music and thought I could be very good": Clinton, *My Life*, p. 63.

4 "I briefly flirted with the idea of dropping out of school": Ibid., p. 104.

5 the delay was a function of ROTC rules: Ibid., p. 155.

5 surely the army would have valued him more for his brains than his brawn: It's true that Yale graduate John Kerry saw frontline action, but he requested—nay, demanded—it.

6 "Then one day, when I was sitting in the back of Professor Emerson's class": Clinton, *My Life*, p. 181.

7   It's a story that has been elaborately, and inaccurately, adorned over the years: The most comical high-drama version of all this was offered by Gail Sheehy in her book *Hillary's Choice* (New York: Random House, 1999), p. 110. In Sheehy's telling, Clinton and her friend Sarah Ehrman, who drove down with her to Arkansas from Washington, arrived in Fayetteville to the horror of seeing a bunch of redneck college students emitting "the high-pitched sound of pigs in heat," chanting "Woo pig suey!" in anticipation of that weekend's Arkansas-Texas football game. Ehrman's shock at this scene is used to drive home the point that Clinton had made a dubious choice. But the Arkansas-Texas game was played October 19 that year, which would have meant that Rodham and Ehrman spent three months driving from Washington to Fayetteville. And besides, the game was played in Texas that year.

7   "He showed up at the Pope County picnic in 1974": Joe Klein, "Bill Clinton: Who Is This Guy?" *New York*, January 20, 1992.

7   "He beat the living hell out of me": Ibid.

8   "It was the single dumbest mistake I ever made in politics until 1994": Clinton, *My Life*, p. 265.

8-9 Then one day in the spring of 1981: Ibid., p. 291.

11   When he finally finished, thirty-three minutes had elapsed: The entire fiasco is available for viewing on YouTube. See https://www .youtube.com/watch?v=vvTRvTII4Oo, or search "Bill Clinton speech Democratic convention 1988."

12   "A little after four o'clock on the afternoon of April 6, 1989": Al From, "Recruiting Bill Clinton," *Atlantic*, December 3, 2013.

12   "We'd leave from Little Rock or maybe Washington": Author interview with Al From, November 9, 2015.

13   "Throughout 1990 and 1991, the DLC plied [Clinton] with critical aid": Kenneth S. Baer, *Reinventing Democrats: The Politics of Liberalism from Reagan to Clinton* (Lawrence: University Press of Kansas, 2000), p. 8.

2. THE COMEBACK KID

16   "We have got to have a message that touches everybody": Quoted in Nick Wing, "Bill Clinton's Clinic: Passionate 1991 Speech Could Show GOP How to Revitalize a Party in Decline," *Huffington Post*, May 24, 2013, http://www.huffingtonpost.com/2013/05/24/bill -clinton-1991-speech_n_3332214.html.

17   "he was the only candidate who had any real stake in its outcome": Richard L. Berke, "Clinton Claims Solid, If Symbolic, Victory in Florida Democrats' Straw Poll," *New York Times*, December 16, 1991.

18   "This is a marriage": Clinton, *My Life*, p. 385. Years later, in his deposition in the Paula Jones sexual harassment case, Clinton acknowledged for the first time (he was under oath) that he'd had an affair with Flowers.

19   "I can't remember if I used the word *meltdown*": Author telephone interview with Stanley Greenberg, November 15, 2015.

20   "What I didn't realize at the time": George Stephanopoulos, *All Too Human: A Political Education* (New York: Back Bay Books, 2000), p. 79.

21   "In our own polls we were in third place": Author telephone interview with Stanley Greenberg.

21   "you might think David Duke was giving that speech": Clinton, *My Life*, p. 411.

22   delegates barked out such names as Archie Bunker and Martha Mitchell: Archie Bunker, of course, was the bigoted protagonist of Norman Lear's *All in the Family*, then a new and sensational hit television show; Mitchell, the wife of Nixon's attorney general and campaign chairman John Mitchell, made frequent and sometimes outrageous statements to the news media, earning the sobriquet "the Mouth of the South" and becoming the target of leaks from the Nixon campaign that she had a drinking problem.

23   with little by way of a credible explanation: Perot said later that he quit because he had heard that the Bush campaign was planning on sabotaging his daughter's wedding.

23   "I think Bush couldn't believe that this guy, this draft dodger, could really beat him": Author telephone interview with Stanley Greenberg.

3. THE NEW REALITIES OF POLITICS

27   Clinton was the second choice of about half of Perot's voters: That Perot cost Bush the election is a piece of conventional wisdom that has lived on ever since, repeated by conservatives and often accepted by liberals because it just sort of seems like it could be true, since Bush and Perot were both more-conservative-than-not (for their time) Texans. But the only study of the matter, based on Perot voters' second choices, found that without Perot in the race, only Ohio would have shifted from Clinton to Bush, still giving Clinton a 349–189 electoral college margin. See, for example, E. J. Dionne Jr., "Perot Seen Not Affecting Vote Outcome," *Washington Post*, November 8, 1992.

27   "deserves the hatred of God": Both Dole and Weyrich are quoted in David Brock, *Blinded by the Right: The Conscience of an Ex-Conservative* (New York: Crown, 2002), p. 147.

28 "keeping this promise will cost you the military": Stephanopoulos, *All Too Human*, p. 123.
29 "You mean to tell me that the success of my program": John Harris, *The Survivor: Bill Clinton in the White House* (New York: Random House Trade Paperbacks, 2006), p. 5.
30 The 1993 deficit was 3.7 percent of the nation's gross domestic product: Economic research of the Federal Reserve Bank of St. Louis, "Federal Surplus or Deficit as Percent of Gross Domestic Product," July 30, 2015, https://research.stlouisfed.org/fred2/series /FYFSGDA188S.
30 "If we didn't get the deficit down substantially": Clinton, *My Life*, p. 461.
33 "When he asked how much time I'd spent on gays in the military": Ibid., p. 520.
34 The Clinton plan left marginal income tax rates the same: The Tax Foundation, "U.S. Federal Individual Income Tax Rates, 1862–2013," October 17, 2013, http://taxfoundation.org/article/us -federal-individual-income-tax-rates-history-1913-2013-nominal -and-inflation-adjusted-brackets.
34 The budget included a 4.3-cent hike in the gasoline tax: See Jodie T. Allen, "The Biggest Tax Increase in History," *Slate*, August 16, 1996, http://www.slate.com/articles/news_and_politics/the _gist/1996/08/the_biggest_tax_increase_in_history.html.
35 "a major antipoverty initiative": V. Joseph Hotz and John Karl Scholz, "The Earned Income Tax Credit," National Bureau of Economic Research, 2003, http://www.nber.org/chapters/c10256.pdf.
35 "an honored place in history": Clinton, *My Life*, p. 536.
35 "As a result of these tactical retreats": Joe Klein, *The Natural: The Misunderstood Presidency of Bill Clinton* (New York: Broadway Books, 2003), p. 55.
36 "At a cabinet meeting, [Bentsen] slammed his fist": Harris, *Survivor*, p. 95.
36 the results of a Gallup poll: "Gallup Poll Finds 46% Opposed, 38% in Favor of NAFTA," *Los Angeles Times*, November 9, 1993.
38 "My instincts were to release the records and fight the prosecutor": Clinton, *My Life*, p. 573.

4. THE LIMITS OF POWER

42 "his campaign has not been able to produce any evidence": "Where Was Clinton on the Gulf War?," *Chicago Tribune*, August 2, 1992.
44 "didn't want to divide the NATO alliance": Clinton, *My Life*, p. 513.
44 "will not stay one day longer than is absolutely necessary": Michael

Wines, "Mission to Somalia: Bush Declares Goal in Somalia to 'Save Thousands,'" *New York Times*, December 5, 1992.

44   "we're being pushed around by these two-bit pricks": Harris, *Survivor*, p. 121.

44   Osama bin Laden made a mental note: It is true that bin Laden marked Mogadishu in his mind. But according to Mark Bowden, the journalist who wrote the definitive account of the Mogadishu firefight, *Black Hawk Down* (New York: Atlantic Monthly Press, 1999), it is not true, as Clinton's critics have asserted over the years, that bin Laden had dispatched al-Qaeda fighters to assist Aidid. See Mark Bowden, "The Truth About Mogadishu," *Philadelphia Inquirer*, October 8, 2006.

47   But over the course of the 1980s, things started to change: See, for example, the Centers for Disease Control, "Health Insurance Coverage Trends, 1959–2007: Estimates from the National Health Interview Survey," *National Health Statistics Reports* 17, July 1, 2009, http://www.cdc.gov/nchs/data/nhsr/nhsr017.pdf.

48   Senate Republican leader Bob Dole was telling him privately: Clinton, *My Life*, p. 547.

49   "in a situation where on health care he never challenged it": Harris, *Survivor*, p. 115.

49   Bentsen personally handed Hillary Clinton a memo: David S. Broder and Haynes Johnson, *The System: The American Way of Politics at the Breaking Point* (New York: Little, Brown, 1996), p. 163.

49   "scathingly dismissed behind their backs": Elizabeth Drew, *On the Edge: The Clinton Presidency* (New York: Simon & Schuster, 1994), p. 305.

50   the changes proposed were indeed vast: The changes proposed were far more extensive than under Barack Obama's Affordable Care Act sixteen years later. To take the most obvious example, "Hillarycare" would have, over time, done away with employer-sponsored coverage entirely by shifting everyone into regional "health alliances." Obamacare had direct impact only on the so-called private market—that is, people who don't have work-sponsored coverage and have to purchase it on their own, which is a small sliver of the overall market.

51   they'd be finished in any bid for reelection: In the House, for example, the vote tally was 235 to 195 in favor. Fully 188 Democrats backed the bill, while 64 Democrats opposed it. About half of those 64 were white members from "gun states" where the NRA could hurt, and about half were liberals, mostly African Americans.

52   "as good as we have a right to expect": Helen Dewar, "Breyer Wins Senate Confirmation to Top Court, 87–9," *Washington Post*, July 30, 1994.

52   "Under the rules of the Senate": Broder and Johnson, *System*, p. 522.
53   "I was pushing the Congress": Clinton, *My Life*, p. 612.

5. THE PRESIDENT IS RELEVANT

55   It was in May 1984: Klein, *Natural*, pp. 89–90.
55   County officials responded by incorporating a new "city": Stepha-
     nie Stokes, "How Atlanta Was Kept Out of Cobb County by a
     10-Foot-Wide City," WABE-FM, April 27, 2015, http://news.wabe
     .org/post/how-atlanta-was-kept-out-cobb-county-10-foot-wide
     -city.
57   a South Carolina mother's drowning of her two young sons: The
     woman's name was Susan Smith; Gingrich's quote was: "The
     mother killing her two children in South Carolina vividly reminds
     every American how sick the society is getting and how much we
     have to have change. I think people want to change and the only
     way you get change is to vote Republican." It later came out that
     Smith had been abused as a girl by a stepfather who was on the
     board of the local Christian Coalition.
57   "Not the House": Harris, *Survivor*, p. 150.
58   The point was not lost on Clinton: Clinton, *My Life*, p. 629.
58   He later reflected that if he'd dropped health care: See ibid., p. 631.
60   "An independent counsel is selected": Quoted in Sidney Blumenthal,
     The Clinton Wars (New York: Farrar, Straus & Giroux, 2003), p. 99.
62   "Go for a head shot": Quoted at Media Matters for America, "Liddy
     Advises Listeners: '[N]o Matter What Law They Pass, Do Not—
     Repeat, Not—Ever Register Any of Your Firearms,'" November 14,
     2008, http://mediamatters.org/video/2008/11/14/liddy-advises
     -listeners-no-matter-what-law-they/146152.
65   "By the time he was killed": Clinton, *My Life*, p. 679.
65   "that would amount to a Republican victory": Harris, *Survivor*, p. 214.
65   "Even if I drop to 5 percent in the polls": Clinton, *My Life*, p. 682.
66   "single most avoidable mistake": Newt Gingrich, *Lessons Learned the
     Hard Way: A Personal Report* (New York: HarperCollins, 1998),
     p. 45.
67   "We made a mistake": Clinton, *My Life*, p. 694.

6. THE CULTURE WARS

71   "Clinton's decision-making process was never truly complete":
     Klein, *Natural*, p. 149.
72   promulgated a few down-the-middle guidelines: Stephen A.
     Holmes, "Clinton Defines Religion's Role in U.S. Schools," *New
     York Times*, August 26, 1995.

72 He defended government racial-preference programs: John Harris, "Clinton Avows Support for Affirmative Action," *Washington Post*, July 20, 1995.

73 "predominantly performed on women": Clinton, *My Life*, p. 706.

75 "The Congress should not use the words 'welfare reform' as a cover": Quoted in "Clinton Vetoes GOP Welfare Reform Bill," *Los Angeles Times*, January 10, 1996.

76 opened the meeting by asking simply, "What should we do?": Harris, *Survivor*, p. 233.

76 "self-consciously statesmanlike": Stephanopoulos, *All Too Human*, p. 420.

77 "This is a decent welfare bill wrapped in a sack of shit": Harris, *Survivor*, p. 238.

77 "If this administration wants to go down in history": Quoted in Robert Gavin, "After a Long Struggle, Welfare Reform—Moynihan's Pleas Ignored Amid Rush to Overhaul," Newhouse News Service, August 11, 1996.

77 "The president has made his decision": Ibid.

80 "scaled-down expectations in domestic policy": Carl Cannon, "Clinton and Top Aides Set Goals for Second Term," *Baltimore Sun*, January 12, 1997.

7. HITTING HIS STRIDE

81 "America's awake": Alison Mitchell, "Clinton Hails Drop in Deficit, Declaring 'America's Awake,'" *New York Times*, October 29, 1996.

81 Median household incomes had gone up: "Median Household Income in the United States," http://www.davemanuel.com /median-household-income.php.

83 "the most permanent feature": Phil Gramm, "Deceptive Budget Deal," *Washington Post*, May 9, 1997.

85 "accomplices in stealing $50,000 from the poor": William Safire, "Partners in Crime?," *New York Times*, May 30, 1996.

85 "when and whether to announce": Jack Nelson, "Starr Will Leave Whitewater Post to Join Pepperdine," *Los Angeles Times*, February 18, 1997.

85 Safire led the charge: William Safire, "The Big Flinch," *New York Times*, February 20, 1997.

86 "concealment and destruction of evidence": Sara Fritz, "Starr Gets More Time for Probe of Whitewater," *Los Angeles Times*, April 23, 1997.

87 these lawyers had come to see the suit: Jill Abramson and Don Van Natta Jr., "Quietly, a Team of Lawyers Kept Paula Jones's Lawsuit Alive," *New York Times*, January 24, 1999.

88 "prove the pundits wrong": Harris, *Survivor*, p. 211.
89 "I pointed out that a declaration that NATO would stop its expansion": Clinton, *My Life*, p. 750.
91 "Clinton felt that he himself was leading an international movement": Blumenthal, *Clinton Wars*, p. 308.

8. THAT WOMAN

93 "to check on the Asian fiscal crisis": Francis X. Clines, "Clinton, in First for a President, Testifies in Sex Harassment Suit," *New York Times*, January 18, 1998.
95 "This could be a problem": Harris, *Survivor*, p. 224.
95 "I also came to understand that when I was exhausted": Clinton, *My Life*, p. 811.
96 "Well, bubeleh": Michael Isikoff, *Uncovering Clinton: A Reporter's Story* (New York: Crown, 1999), p. 196.
97 "There are lots of us busy elves": Ibid., p. 182.
97 against the standards of journalism in which he was trained: Ibid., p. 204.
98 "first-class media hound": David Plotz, "Susan Carpenter-McMillan: The Woman Who Ate Paula Jones," *Slate*, September 21, 1997.
99 "After Goldberg finished telling Tripp's story": Joe Conason and Gene Lyons, *The Hunting of the President: The Ten-Year Campaign to Destroy Bill and Hillary Clinton* (New York: St. Martin's Press, 2001), p. 339.
100 "inchoate criminality": Isikoff, *Uncovering Clinton*, p. 304.
100 "Ma'am, you are in serious trouble": Andrew Morton, *Monica's Story* (New York: St. Martin's Press, 1999), Kindle version, location 324.
101 "whether Clinton and his close friend Vernon Jordan": Peter Baker, Toni Locy, and Susan Schmidt, "Clinton Accused of Urging Aide to Lie," *Washington Post*, January 21, 1998.
103 "as the military aide announced his name": Hillary Clinton, *Living History* (New York: Simon & Schuster, 2003), p. 449.
103 William Ginsburg, who instantly became a ubiquitous television presence: Ginsburg gave his name to an only-in-Washington phenomenon: after his moment in the spotlight, anyone appearing on all five major Sunday shows on the same day was thenceforth referred to as doing "a full Ginsburg."
103 "This is the great story here": Blumenthal, *Clinton Wars*, p. 374.
104 "After the story broke, I called [lawyer] David Kendall": Clinton, *My Life*, p. 775.
106 The president's approval rating had risen to 73 percent: Blumenthal, *Clinton Wars*, p. 425.

107 "one of the happiest days of my presidency": Clinton, *My Life*, p. 784.

107 "They have had me for twenty-seven years": Ibid., p. 783.

108 "a previously unknown group called the Liberation Army of the Islamic Sanctuaries": James C. McKinley Jr., "Two U.S. Embassies in East Africa Are Bombed," *New York Times*, August 8, 1998.

109 "to be run out of office in the flood tide": Clinton, *My Life*, p. 800.

110 "it was unnaturally dark, with rain pelting the windows": Michael Waldman, *POTUS Speaks* (New York: Simon & Schuster, 2000), p. 227.

110 "You're the one who got yourself into this mess": Hillary Clinton, *Living History*, p. 468.

110 "I did have a relationship with Miss Lewinsky": Blumenthal, *Clinton Wars*, p. 465.

9. UNBREAKABLE

114 "Mr. President, we are going to run you out of town": Harris, *Survivor*, p. 334.

114 "I think the president did exactly the right thing today": Quoted in Micah Zenko, "How Risky Was the Osama bin Laden Raid?," Council on Foreign Relations, April 30, 2012.

114 "would have been derelict in our duty": James Risen, "To Bomb Sudan Plant, or Not: A Year Later, Debates Rankle," *New York Times*, October 27, 1999.

114 "credible military leader": Keating Holland, "Most Americans Support Sudan, Afghanistan Strikes," CNN.com, August 21, 1998.

115 The word *sex* (or some variation thereof) appeared 581 times; the word *Whitewater* four times: Hillary Clinton, *Living History*, p. 475.

116 "I don't think there is a fancy way to say that I have sinned": "Transcript: Clinton Speaks to Prayer Breakfast," CNN.com, September 11, 1998.

116 "Until it was measured by Kenneth Starr, no citizen": "Shame at the White House," *New York Times*, September 12, 1998.

117 "Representative Hyde sought to strike a lofty tone": Brian Knowlton, "U.S. House Votes, 258–176, for Clinton Impeachment Inquiry," *New York Times*, October 9, 1998.

120 Black turnout was especially high for a midterm election: According to figures compiled by the U.S. Census Bureau, black turnout in 1998 was 39.6 percent, and white turnout was 43.3 percent. So white turnout was still higher, but it was down from 47.3 percent in 1994, the previous midterm election, while black turnout was just 37.1 percent in 1994. See Census Bureau, "Voting and Registration in the Election of November 1998," P20-523RV.

120   "Years ago, in the middle of the Whitewater investigation": Toni Morrison, Comment, *New Yorker*, October 5, 1998.
125   "to be a repairer of the breach": Alison Mitchell, "Clinton Impeached; He Faces a Senate Trial, 2nd in U.S. History; Vows to Do Job Till Term's 'Last Hour,'" *New York Times*, December 20, 1998.

10. DUCKING LIGHTNING BOLTS TILL THE END

129   "she was going to have to be talked out of it": Michael Tomasky, *Hillary's Turn: Inside Her Improbable, Victorious Senate Campaign* (New York: Free Press, 2001), pp. 44–45.
130   "if that particular technical annex was something that bothered them": Barnaby Mason, "Rambouillet Talks 'Designed to Fail,'" BBC News, March 19, 2000.
131   "I apologized again and told him I was sure": Clinton, *My Life*, p. 855.
132   "gave away the store": "White House Blunders on Environment Bills," *Seattle Post-Intelligencer*, December 4, 1995.
132   "set aside more acreage under the Act than Theodore Roosevelt": Paul Wapner, "Clinton's Environmental Legacy," *Tikkun*, March/April 2001, p. 11.
133   "if he was satisfied with the Jerusalem question": Clinton, *My Life*, p. 914.
134   "a better idea of each side's bottom line": Ibid., p. 916.
135   "openly brags about its support for a Mideast terrorism group": Tomasky, *Hillary's Turn*, p. 270.
136   "It was an appalling decision": Clinton, *My Life*, p. 933.
137   "I am not a great man": Ibid., p. 944.
138   "The trailer-trash Clintons and their staff": Eric Boehlert, "The White House Vandal Scandal That Wasn't," *Salon*, May 23, 2001.
139   "there is no record of damage": Ibid.

EPILOGUE

141   "He would promise to stop": Joe Conason, *Man of the World: The Further Endeavors of Bill Clinton* (New York: Simon & Schuster, 2016), p. 15.
143   figuring out this new TiVo: See David A. Farenthold, Tom Hamburger, and Rosalind S. Helderman, "The Inside Story of How the Clintons Built a $2 Billion Empire," *Washington Post*, June 2, 2015.
144   turned him down cold: Conason, *Man of the World*, p. 94.
149   "The Clinton project in national governance": Ed Kilgore, "The End of the Clinton Era of Democratic Politics," *New York*, November 10, 2016.

Milestones

1946 Bill Clinton is born William Jefferson Blythe III in Hope, Arkansas, on August 19. His father, William Jefferson Blythe Jr., had died in a car crash four months earlier.

1950 Virginia Blythe, his mother, marries Roger Clinton; mother and son take Roger's surname.

1953 Family moves from Hope to Hot Springs.

1963 Attends American Legion Boys Nation event in Washington, D.C., and shakes hands with President John F. Kennedy.

1964 Starts college at the Edmund A. Walsh School of Foreign Service, Georgetown University.

1966 Begins working part-time for Senator J. William Fulbright.

1968 Graduates from Georgetown; is named a Rhodes scholar and attends University College, Oxford.

1969 Tells Colonel Eugene Holmes, who headed the University of Arkansas Army Reserve Officers' Training Corps (ROTC), that he would attend law school at Fayetteville when he finished at Oxford and join the ROTC.

After drawing a high number in the draft lottery five months later, writes to Holmes to thank him for "saving me from the draft," noting that he had initially decided to accept the draft despite his opposition to the war to "maintain my political viability within the system."

1970 Starts law school at Yale University.

1971 Meets fellow Yale law student Hillary Diane Rodham.

1972 Works on his first political campaign, helping to coordinate the campaign in Texas for Democratic presidential nominee George McGovern.

1973   Graduates from Yale Law School; returns to Arkansas.

1974   Runs for Congress, narrowly losing to Republican incumbent John Paul Hammerschmidt.

1975   Marries Hillary Rodham on October 11.

1976   Elected attorney general of Arkansas.

1978   Elected governor of Arkansas, becoming the nation's youngest governor at thirty-two.

1980   Daughter Chelsea Victoria Clinton is born in Little Rock on February 27.

Loses reelection bid, the last election he ever lost.

1982   Elected governor once again.

1985   Al From founds the centrist Democratic Leadership Council (DLC), with which Clinton is affiliated from the beginning.

1986   Becomes chair of the National Governors Association.

1988   Delivers nominating speech for Michael Dukakis at the Democratic National Convention.

1989   Becomes chairman of the DLC and travels the country to lay groundwork for future presidential bid.

1991   Announces candidacy for president.

1992   Gennifer Flowers story breaks and draft story is revealed; Clinton finishes second in New Hampshire primary and dubs himself "the Comeback Kid."

Rebukes Jesse Jackson at Rainbow PUSH Coalition meeting for hosting rapper Sister Souljah.

Receives Democratic presidential nomination in July and chooses Senator Al Gore as his running mate.

Wins presidency in November, defeating incumbent president George Herbert Walker Bush.

1993   Sworn in as forty-second president of the United States on January 20; is immediately enmeshed in gays-in-the-military controversy.

Nominates Ruth Bader Ginsburg to the U.S. Supreme Court.

Budget passes by one vote in each house of Congress, raising some taxes to promote deficit reduction and investment.

Hosts Israeli prime minister Yitzhak Rabin and Palestinian leader Yasser Arafat at White House on September 13.

Announces health care reform effort, to be led by Hillary Clinton.

Congress passes North American Free Trade Agreement (NAFTA) and Brady gun-control bill.

1994   Attorney General Janet Reno names special prosecutor Robert B. Fiske Jr. to look into allegations around the Whitewater land deal.

Paula Jones files sexual harassment lawsuit against Clinton about an alleged 1991 incident.

Nominates Stephen Breyer to the U.S. Supreme Court.

Congress passes crime bill with money for 100,000 more police officers, death penalties for more federal crimes, and some social spending for youth.

Health care reform effort dies.

Republican congressional leaders and candidates issue the Contract with America, outlining their policy priorities for the midterm elections.

Approves use of force to restore Jean-Bertrand Aristide to the presidency of Haiti.

Republicans sweep midterm elections in November and take control of both House and Senate.

1995   Newt Gingrich becomes Speaker of the House.

Oklahoma City terrorist bombing occurs on April 19, killing 168.

Special judicial panel fires Fiske and replaces him with Kenneth Starr.

Yitzhak Rabin is assassinated.

First government showdown over budget impasse occurs in November; Clinton begins affair with Monica Lewinsky.

Dayton Agreement is signed, outlining peace in Bosnia.

1996   Second government shutdown leads to budget agreement on Clinton's terms.

Physical contact with Lewinsky ends in March.

Signs welfare reform bill with strict new work requirements and devolution of authority to states.

Wins reelection in November, defeating Senator Bob Dole.

1997   Agrees to long-term deal with Gingrich and Senate majority leader Trent Lott to balance the budget.

Supreme Court rules unanimously that Paula Jones's lawsuit against Clinton may proceed.

Paula Jones parts ways with lawyers, teams up with conservative Rutherford Institute; Linda Tripp begins tape recording conversations with Lewinsky.

1998   News of the Clinton-Lewinsky affair breaks in mid-January; Clinton delivers tense State of the Union address.

Al-Qaeda bombs U.S. embassies in Kenya and Tanzania on August 7.

Clinton gives grand jury testimony to Starr on August 17.

Orders bombing of suspected al-Qaeda operations on August 19 in retaliation for embassy bombings.

Starr report is made public on September 11.

House of Representatives opens impeachment inquiry on October 8.

Hosts Wye River conference in an effort to restart Middle East peace talks.

House votes to impeach Clinton on December 19.

1999   Senate impeachment trial begins on January 7; Clinton is acquitted on all charges on February 12.

NATO begins bombing of Belgrade to halt Serbian aggression in Kosovo.

Hillary Clinton begins campaign for New York's U.S. Senate seat.

2000   Camp David meetings with Yasser Arafat and Israeli prime minister Ehud Barak.

Vice President Gore receives Democratic nomination for president.

Al-Qaeda attacks USS *Cole* in Aden harbor, Yemen.

Hillary Clinton wins election to the U.S. Senate; Al Gore and George W. Bush are locked in a recount in Florida.

Supreme Court decides *Bush v. Gore* on December 12, handing presidency to Bush.

2001 Clinton's final effort at Middle East peace fails as Arafat walks away.

George W. Bush is sworn in as president.

Moves to New York and establishes the William J. Clinton Foundation.

2004 Publishes his autobiography, *My Life*.

Undergoes emergency heart bypass surgery.

2008 Hillary Clinton pursues Democratic presidential nomination but falls short.

2009 President Barack Obama names Hillary Clinton secretary of state.

2015 Hillary Clinton announces presidential campaign.

2016 Donald Trump defeats Hillary Clinton in the presidential election.

Selected Bibliography

Baer, Kenneth S. *Reinventing Democrats: The Politics of Liberalism from Reagan to Clinton.* Lawrence: University Press of Kansas, 2000.

Bernstein, Carl. *A Woman in Charge: The Life of Hillary Rodham Clinton.* New York: Alfred A. Knopf, 2007.

Blumenthal, Sidney. *The Clinton Wars.* New York: Farrar, Straus and Giroux, 2003.

Boys, James D. *Clinton's Grand Strategy: U.S. Foreign Policy in a Post–Cold War World.* New York: Bloomsbury Academic, 2015.

Brock, David. *Blinded by the Right: The Conscience of an Ex-Conservative.* New York: Crown, 2002.

Broder, David S., and Haynes Johnson. *The System: The American Way of Politics at the Breaking Point.* New York: Little, Brown, 1996.

Chollet, Derek, and Samantha Power, eds. *The Unquiet American: Richard Holbrooke in the World.* New York: PublicAffairs, 2011.

Clinton, Bill. *My Life.* New York: Alfred A. Knopf, 2004.

Clinton, Hillary. *Living History.* New York: Simon & Schuster, 2003.

Conason, Joe. *Man of the World: The Further Endeavors of Bill Clinton.* New York: Simon & Schuster, 2016.

——— and Gene Lyons. *The Hunting of the President: The Ten-Year Campaign to Destroy Bill and Hillary Clinton.* New York: St. Martin's Press, 2001.

Drew, Elizabeth. *On the Edge: The Clinton Presidency.* New York: Simon & Schuster, 1994.

From, Al. *The New Democrats and the Return to Power.* New York: St. Martin's, 2013.

Gerth, Jeff, and Don Van Natta Jr. *Her Way: The Hopes and Ambitions of Hillary Rodham Clinton*. New York: Little, Brown, 2007.

Gingrich, Newt. *Lessons Learned the Hard Way: A Personal Report*. New York: HarperCollins, 1998.

Harris, John. *The Survivor: Bill Clinton in the White House*. New York: Random House Trade Paperbacks, 2006.

Hyland, William G. *Clinton's World: Remaking American Foreign Policy*. Westport, Conn.: Praeger, 1999.

Isikoff, Michael. *Uncovering Clinton: A Reporter's Story*. New York: Crown, 1999.

Klein, Joe. *The Natural: The Misunderstood Presidency of Bill Clinton*. New York: Broadway Books, 2003.

Maraniss, David. *First in His Class: A Biography of Bill Clinton*. New York: Simon & Schuster, 1996.

McDougal, Susan, with Pat Harris. *The Woman Who Wouldn't Talk: Why I Refused to Testify Against the Clintons and What I Learned in Jail*. New York: Carroll & Graf, 2002.

Morris, Roger. *Partners in Power: The Clintons and Their America*. New York: Henry Holt, 1996.

Morton, Andrew. *Monica's Story*. New York: St. Martin's Press, 1999.

Olson, Barbara. *Hell to Pay: The Unfolding Story of Hillary Rodham Clinton*. Washington, D.C.: Regnery, 1999.

Panetta, Leon. *Worthy Fights: A Memoir of Leadership in War and Peace*. New York: Penguin Press, 2014.

Reich, Robert B. *Locked in the Cabinet*. New York: Alfred A. Knopf, 1997.

Ross, Dennis. *Doomed to Succeed: The U.S.-Israel Relationship from Truman to Obama*. New York: Farrar, Straus and Giroux, 2015.

Rubin, Robert, with Jacob Weisberg. *In an Uncertain World: Tough Choices from Wall Street to Washington*. New York: Random House, 2003.

Ruddy, Christopher. *The Strange Death of Vincent Foster: An Investigation*. New York: Free Press, 1997.

Sheehy, Gail. *Hillary's Choice*. New York: Random House, 1999.

Smith, Sally Bedell. *For Love of Politics: Bill and Hillary Clinton: The White House Years*. New York: Random House, 2007.

Starr, Kenneth. *The Starr Report: The Findings of Independent Counsel Kenneth W. Starr on President Clinton and the Lewinsky Affair*. New York: PublicAffairs, 1998.

Stephanopoulos, George. *All Too Human: A Political Education.* New York: Back Bay Books, 2000.

Talbott, Strobe. *The Russia Hand: A Memoir of Presidential Diplomacy.* New York: Random House, 2002.

Tomasky, Michael. *Hillary's Turn: Inside Her Improbable, Victorious Senate Campaign.* New York: Free Press, 2001.

Toobin, Jeffrey. *A Vast Conspiracy: The Real Story of the Sex Scandal That Nearly Brought Down a President.* New York: Random House, 1999.

Tyrrell, R. Emmett, Jr. *Boy Clinton: The Political Biography.* Washington, D.C.: Regnery, 1996.

Waldman, Michael. *POTUS Speaks: Finding the Words That Defined the Clinton Presidency.* New York: Simon & Schuster, 2000.

Woodward, Bob. *The Agenda: Inside the Clinton White House.* New York: Simon & Schuster, 1994.

Acknowledgments

I have known Sean Wilentz for about twenty years and have respected his work for much longer. It was an honor to be asked by Sean to contribute the Bill Clinton entry in the American Presidents series. I should add a posthumous tribute to the great Arthur M. Schlesinger Jr., who started this series and whom I was privileged to get to know a bit toward the end of his life. I hope I have done him honor.

I also met Paul Golob close to two decades ago. He signed me in 1999 to write a book about that other Clinton, Hillary, and her improbable Senate race. Between the time I signed the contract and delivered the manuscript, Paul had taken another job, so we never did get to work together. I'm happy we were able to correct this and am deeply grateful to him, and to Sean, for their perceptive comments.

My agent, Chris Calhoun, is a dear friend—and a very smart reader in his own right. I thank Chris for his work and his sharp comments on the manuscript.

A few old Clinton hands, including Stan Greenberg and Al From, shared thoughts with me on the record. Many others, as well as a few journalists, spoke with me on background to offer their insights. I thank them all.

I thank my wife, Sarah Kerr, for all her support; and finally there's dear young Margot, who keeps me going and gets me out of bed in the morning—figuratively and, most days, literally.

Index

ABOUT THE AUTHOR

MICHAEL TOMASKY is a special correspondent for the *Daily Beast* and the editor in chief of *Democracy: A Journal of Ideas*, as well as a regular contributor to the *New York Review of Books*. He was previously executive editor of the *American Prospect* and was the first U.S. editor of the *Guardian*. He is the author of *Left for Dead: The Life, Death, and Possible Resurrection of Progressive Politics in America*; *Hillary's Turn: Inside Her Improbable, Victorious Senate Campaign*; and the ebook *Yeah! Yeah! Yeah!: The Beatles and America, Then and Now*. He lives outside Washington, D.C.